HOW TO

lose weight *and* GAIN MONEY

A PROGRAM FOR PUTTING YOUR LIFE IN ORDER

HOW TO

lose weight *and*
GAIN MONEY

A PROGRAM FOR PUTTING YOUR LIFE IN ORDER

Vivien S. Schapera • Drew A. Logan

Four Winds Press LLC

CINCINNATI, OHIO

This book is designed to provide readers with a program for putting their life in order by looking at their existing patterns and altering them in accordance with desired results. It is not designed to be a definitive guide to either investment or health and should not take the place of professional advice from suitably qualified financial or health advisors. Thus neither the publisher nor the authors assume liability of any kind for any losses that may be sustained as a result of applying the methods suggested in this book, and any such liability is hereby expressly disclaimed.

ISBN: 0-9709809-5-7

Library of Congress Cataloging-in-Publication Data:

Not available at time of printing

Dedication

To my parents, Frank and Betty, who encouraged my love of reading which led to my love of writing.

— Drew

To my brother, Michael, and my uncle Harry. who taught me how to enjoy money and how to enjoy food.

— Vivien

Acknowledgments

Drew — Thank you for teaching me the meaning of true partnership in the writing of this book.

Vivien — What you have taught me about book writing, pales in comparison to what you have allowed me to learn about myself.

Our sincere thanks go to the following people for their valued expertise:

Kevin — for visionary editing and guidance

Kathleen — for masterful cover art and book design

Stephanie — for untiring research and project planning

Nancy — for your listening ear and practical solutions

Neil — for your affirming attitude and web site support

Contents

Chapter 2 continued
What's Your Story?

Chapter 3
Where Are You?   47

Chapter 4
Where Are You Headed?   57

Chapter 8
Will You Reach Your Destination?

Chapter 9
Keeping Life in Balance

Appendices

1

the link
between weight and money

"I don't want the cheese,
 I just want to get out of the trap."

Spanish Proverb

If you want to spend the rest of your life in distress about your waistline and your bank balance, put this book down now. But, if you're ready to put your life in order, read on.

This is a serious program, which will teach you how to reverse the downward spiral of weight gain and money loss, destructive in your own life, and plaguing our nation.

Our Lose Weight, Gain Money℠ program builds the framework necessary to support successful weight loss and financial management in your life, by teaching you how to:

○ Understand the significance of seeing yourself as an individual

○ Discover your patterns of behavior

○ Ascertain the results of your existing patterns

○ Accomplish the changes you desire

○ Reach your goals and maintain balance in your life

We are not recommending a specific diet. Nor are we promoting an investment strategy. What we will do is ease you step-by-step through the basics of universal methods of financial management and help you choose a diet program that is suited to your individual needs. We will provide you with references and resources and show you how to integrate all this information into your life.

We will also explain to you why, even though you might already know how to lose weight or gain money, you haven't yet been able to apply what you know. And, if you already are successful in either weight loss or money gain, this program will help you apply your methods of success in money gain to weight loss and vice-versa.

Is Any of the Following Familiar ...?

It's been a hard day. The traffic jam made you late for work, preventing you from doing that all-important last minute preparation for your meeting. Then the bank called, asking you to come in and sign the papers again, because there was a clerical error, and please could you come before Tuesday. You have no idea how you're going to get time off to do that. And oh no! You forgot to call the contractor about the water in the basement, so that will have to wait until Monday — which means it will be too late to save the carpet.

To make matters worse, you've been waking up in the middle of the night, wondering how you're going to pay the bills, juggle the commitments of the weekend and see your aunt who has recently been hospitalized. If only you didn't have the children's sports commitments peppering Saturday and Sunday and your friend's party on Saturday night. You don't want to miss the party — it's just that you don't know how you're going to prepare the dish you promised *and* get to the party before midnight.

It is Friday evening and you've taken the family shopping. You're looking at washing machines. It's time to replace the fourteen-year-old machine that came with the house. There are too many choices and you can't clear your mind to make a decision. You resolve not to make any purchases until you've figured out how much money you still owe on your credit cards. With all the recent emergencies, the credit card balances have crept up and you're under pressure to make the payments.

You look around for your children. One is over in the TV section looking at plasma screens, another is looking at MP3 players. As you walk over, the begging begins: "Please can I have ..."

"No," you say, "not tonight."

"But all my friends ..."

"No, no, NO!" you say firmly, "we can't afford to buy more stuff. Not right now. I'm not even getting the washing machine we need."

That's when your eye falls on the digital camera. The floor model is on sale for $300 less than the original price — a once in a lifetime opportunity. You turn the camera over in your hands. For six months you've been needing a digital camera to finish your web site. What a bargain. If you don't snap up the camera now, someone else will. You stand lost in your desire to own this camera.

This is your chance to get what you want, fulfill your own dream. The reduced price seems like a sign indicating that you are meant to have this camera. An unsolicited credit card arrived in the mail a few days ago — you can use that to make the purchase. The "what-about-your budget?" voice recedes. You'll manage somehow. You've always managed to make your payments and besides, your parents usually give you money for your birthday, which is coming up in less than two months. You march up to the desk and buy the camera.

You feel quite heady now. What a good week this has been after all. Having a bargain fall into your lap is just what you needed to turn your mood around. You've been planning this purchase for ages. This is the opposite of impulse buying. You're definitely being sensible.

"Let's go celebrate," you say, "who wants a brownie sundae?"

"I do, I do," say the kids.

And you think to yourself, "I'm going to have one of those fancy coffee drinks I've been threatening to try, as well." Since you're breaking your diet, you may as well really indulge.

You all enjoy the sweet taste of success. The tense week has ended with a fun evening out. You look at the smiling faces of your family. You don't even mind the $30 check, because that can go on the new credit card too.

That is, you don't mind until thirty days later, when the bill arrives and you wake up in the night wondering how you're going to pay ...

If any part of this story sounds familiar, you are participating in a growing national trend.

As a nation, our behavior with regard to weight and money is, frankly, out of control. It is frightening how much money the average American family needs — or thinks it needs — to get by. We are a nation of consumers.

Take a moment to look at the contents of your refrigerator and your pantry. How much of your food is nutritionally necessary? Have you wondered recently why you can't lose weight?

Have you wondered recently where all your money is going? Take a look around at your personal possessions. How many of them do you use regularly? Are they all necessary for you to function in life?

We are a nation indulging in excess consumption and when things aren't going our way, we comfort ourselves by consuming more.

The Weight Gain Money Loss Insight

'Twas a dark and stormy summer. Wind pummeled the trees, lightning cracked at the windows. In the spring, tornadoes had ripped through the country. One and a half years earlier, terrorists had steered planes into the World Trade Center. The stock market had plummeted. The percentage of joblessness had risen to the highest level in nine years.

The executive team of our non-profit school had planned a five-day conference and registration numbers were 75% under what we'd hoped. Across the country, similar conferences were being canceled due to lack of attendance. We'd already invested a substantial amount of time and money and we did not want to sustain a loss *and* have nothing to show for it.

"This sucks," Vivien said, thinking of her personal situation. "I'm gaining weight and losing money, instead of the other way round! We need to reverse this."

That's when we got it. Weight loss and money gain are not the same thing, but they are related. All we had to do was look at the national situation to confirm our insight. Newspapers were simultaneously reporting the rise of obesity and the fall of the dollar.

Does that mean that fat people lose money? No, not exactly, but in that moment we could see the bridge linking these two issues. As further confirmation, we flashed on what every woman knows — when she's anxious, food helps. And shopping does too.

There is something very comforting about consumption whether it be spending money or indulging in a favorite food treat.

You are probably wondering who "We" are. Let us take a moment for introductions. Vivien is the chair and founder of FourWinds Academy for the Healing Arts and Sciences. She is a psychologist, an Alexander teacher, a healer, a writer, a personal coach and a martial arts instructor. She practices all of these professions under the umbrella of "teacher."

Drew volunteers as a board member and business/finance director for FourWinds Academy. He retired from the banking industry at the age of 41. He now spends his time teaching, writing and helping people with their finances.

Some of this book we have written from joint perceptions and some from personal experience. We have freely used "I" and "We" to refer to ourselves. Since Vivien is female, married and has two children and Drew is male and has the banking background, we believe the reader will easily ascertain, from the content, who is speaking.

We are going to combine our two fields of expertise to bring you this revolutionary program: **Lose Weight, Gain Money**^{SM}.

Let's begin!

First let us show you the bridge between weight gain and money loss.

The Behavioral Bridge Between Weight Gain and Money Loss

Weight gain and money loss are due to:

- Excessive Consumption

- Imbalance between what's coming in and what's going out

- Loss of Control (including disrupted energy and lack of self-discipline)

- Comfort Seeking (including addictions, bingeing and self-medication)

- Genetics and Family Patterns

- Environmental Influences, including peer pressure, fashion and trends

- Faulty equations in which Money = Love and Food = Love

Here is a startling fact. The United States is the richest nation in the world but we have one of the lowest rates of personal savings of all the industrialized nations. As a nation, we continue to manifest an international trade deficit, which means, basically, we continue to spend more than we take in.

Another puzzler is that we have access to every opportunity to lead a healthy lifestyle, yet 2/3 of our adults are overweight. And our children are following in our heavy footsteps.

We cannot deny that the people of the United States of America are sharing a group consciousness. We are a world power blessed with great accomplishments. However, there is no light without shadow, and the shadow side of our culture rears an ugly head when it comes to issues of consumption.

Studies regularly compare the diet, drinking and smoking habits of the French with the diet, drinking and smoking habits of North Americans and come up with baffling results. What such studies can't and haven't taken into account is the difference in the national consciousness of the French and the Americans.

What will help each of us, as individuals, is comprehending how we are influenced by our culture. We are being dragged by the current, bobbing up and down under the influence of the reigning energy.

The Collective Unconscious

Our nation has been under assault. Let's make a list of the events which have dominated our group consciousness since 2001:

- ○ Terrorist attack
- ○ War in Afghanistan
- ○ Stock market crash
- ○ Falling dollar

- ○ War in Iraq
- ○ Threatened economy
- ○ Natural disasters, floods and tornadoes
- ○ Rise in Joblessness

It is time for us to face the horrible fact that, if we want to be different from the national trend, we are going to have to take personal action to change. The moment we make that decision, the rest will follow.

> "Nothing has changed but my attitude, therefore, everything has changed."
>
> Anthony DeMello

"Why?" not "How?"

The strange truth is that we all know many answers that will solve our problems. Here are two well-known approaches to losing weight and gaining money: To lose weight, eat less and exercise more. To gain money, spend less than you earn and invest your savings.

We even know what will and won't work for us personally. But something is stopping us. **The answer is simple, but not easy**. The real question in not "how?" but "why?"

○ Why can't I lose weight? ○ Why can't I gain money?

Especially since you do know how! The answers lie inside you. The exercises in this book, especially those in Chapter 2, will help you discover the answers to **all** of the following questions:

○ Why do I gain weight? ○ Why do I lose money?
○ Why don't I lose weight? ○ Why don't I gain money?

Personal Patterns

Have you ever watched in frustration as a friend turns everything she touches into gold while what you touch crumbles to dust? Do you have a sibling that has been generating money since he was a teenager, while you just can't figure it out?

Do you have a friend that can eat anything she likes, while the mere act of sniffing a piece of chocolate cake puts pounds on you? Have you gone running for miles and miles, dieted carefully and lost one pound after three weeks, while your husband has lost five pounds in one week, eating the same meals?

Life just doesn't seem fair. Well, it isn't. Maybe there is such a thing as a lucky star. If there is a lucky star — and you weren't born under it — that doesn't mean you're doomed. There is plenty you can do about it.

Hidden inside and around us are layers and layers of information. Systematic exploration will reveal the hidden causes of your behavior and patterns, which frustrate your efforts to put your life in order. We are going to look at those layers, chapter by chapter.

It is time for you to begin reversing your negative spiral of weight gain and money loss. Here is the behavioral bridge with the positive qualities added. You will want your new behavior to be guided by these positive qualities.

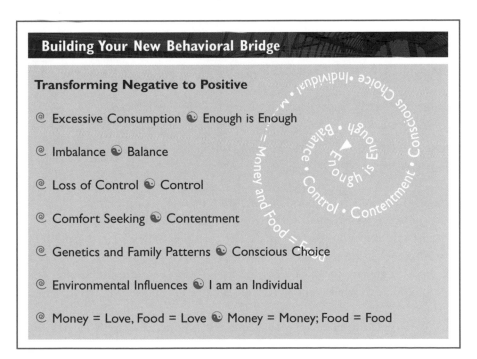

Building Your New Behavioral Bridge

Transforming Negative to Positive

- Excessive Consumption ☯ Enough is Enough

- Imbalance ☯ Balance

- Loss of Control ☯ Control

- Comfort Seeking ☯ Contentment

- Genetics and Family Patterns ☯ Conscious Choice

- Environmental Influences ☯ I am an Individual

- Money = Love, Food = Love ☯ Money = Money; Food = Food

To Follow The Program

1. Get a pen, pencil, eraser, journal or binder, a pocket-sized notebook and calculator.

2. Assess your style:
   * Read the whole book to get an overview, then do the program
   * Read and do the program as you go
   * Combo: read and do "a rough draft" of the program, then go back and refine.

   Whatever your style, **you will have to do the program** to get the benefits. Passively understanding the insights will not yield results. Actively participating in the process and changing your patterns will.

   If your style is to read the whole book first, make yourself a promise now to go back and do the program.

3. You will have to choose a diet program that suits your individual tastes. This will require some research. If you want to get a head start on doing that research, look at the following possibilities:

   ○ Low fat ○ Dean Ornish ○ Eat Right for Your Type ○ Vegetarian

   ○ Macrobiotic ○ Ayurvedic ○ Organic/Whole Foods ○ Weight Watchers®

   ○ Atkins™/South Beach ○ 5 Day Miracle Diet (Adele Puhn)

   These are not recommendations. Get medical advice before beginning a new diet.

   Each of these diets is included because they are lifestyle programs that will teach you a way of eating for the rest of your life. Every diet requires you to give up certain foods. For example, in Atkins you give up refined carbohydrates, in Weight Watchers you give up quantity, in a vegetarian diet you give up meat, poultry and fish. You will need to match the diet of your choice to what you can realistically give up in the long term.

4. We supply the financial management techniques that apply to everyone and "Quick Charts" are provided to replace calculations.

5. We recommend that you consolidate all of the information for both weight loss and money gain in your journal. To get copies of the financial worksheets, you can either photocopy from the book or download from our website and then paste them into the journal.

6. Sequencing: In some cases, it is obvious that a step needs to be completed before another step can be taken. Other steps require ongoing process and do not have to be completed before continuing with another step. If it is not obvious, there is no required sequence.

7. Some steps will yield immediate results, others yield medium or long-term gains. Together, all the steps will affect the rest of your life.

8. We supply approximate time guidelines for each exercise. Take as long as you need.

9. It will take approximately twelve weeks to put the initial building blocks of the program in place. You should be able to look back and see measur-able progress at three-month intervals and rewarding changes after a year. Sustaining the program will continue to yield a lifetime of results.

10. Right about now, you may be asking yourself "If I don't need to lose weight, but have money challenges (or vice-versa), do I have to participate in both sections of the program?" The answer is "Yes."

Remember the behavioral bridge between weight gain and money loss? At the end of each chapter, mindfully review what you have written with regard to the money exercises and what you have written with regard to the weight exercises, and then:

A Analyze the similarities and differences in your weight and money patterns

C Choose the patterns which bring you success

T Transfer your methods of success with regard to weight to money and your methods of success with money to weight

 Becoming an Individual Again

Exercise 1.1: Assess Your Tendencies (20 minutes)

Weight gain and money loss are a result of lifestyle.

Which of the elements of the behavioral bridge between weight gain and money loss are mostly inherent in your individual make-up and which of them have come about mostly because you are sharing the American lifestyle? Write an "I" next to your individual tendencies write an "S" next to your socially induced tendencies. (None of these elements will be purely individual or social. Estimate which influence is stronger. The point of the exercise is reflection and insight, not "being right.")

M | W

_____ Excessive Consumption

_____ Imbalance between what's coming in and what's going out

_____ Loss of Control (including disrupted energy and lack of self-discipline)

_____ Comfort Seeking (including addictions, binging and self-medication)

_____ Genetics and Family Patterns

_____ Environmental Influences, including peer pressure, fashion and trends

_____ Faulty equations in which Money = Love and Food = Love

Take your journal and make quick comments on each of the above elements, noting how these elements apply to you personally. For example:

_S | I_ Excessive consumption

W: "I am always aware of what I eat, no matter who I am with or where I am."

M: "I am quite careful about my shopping habits when I am on my own, but when I go shopping with a friend, I tend to get carried away."

Becoming an Individual Again

Exercise 1.2: Coping Strategies (30 minutes)

You need to take back the reins and start making lifestyle choices compatible with your individuality. This requires strategy and sometimes a step-by-step approach of instituting the strategy, because the people around us tend to resent our changes and feel more comfortable when we stay in the fold.

1. Make notes of all the places you notice yourself being dragged by the current in either your eating patterns, your spending patterns or both:

   Work   Keeping up with the
                                 neighbors
   Social get-togethers
                                 Reacting to commercials
   Family get-togethers
                                 Reacting to bargains/sales
   Fashion

2. Make a few notes about strategies you can employ and how you can begin to institute them.

3. Keep your eyes and ears open for new ideas.

4. Speak to others who are trying to solve the same kinds of problems.

5. Ask yourself "What would **I** choose if it were just up to me?"

For example:

○ If you prefer to bring your own lunch to work rather than eat in a restaurant with your co-workers, find a way to eat your home-prepared meal. You will save money and calories. No need to be anti-social. At lunchtime you can drink a cup of tea while your friends eat. After a week or two, your friends will probably want to join you on the program.

○ If a friend asks you to go shopping with her, don't feel obligated to go unless you have something specific in mind to purchase. There is no reason to put yourself in the way of temptation.

Exercise 1.2 CONTINUED

○ If there is a custom of bringing cakes and cookies to work and you want to break the sugar habit, bring your bag of celery. When it is your turn to provide the food, stick to a sensible budget and provide healthy fare. You won't be wasting money on food that everyone will wish later they hadn't eaten.

○ Just because your children like to eat pizza on Monday nights after soccer practice, doesn't mean you have to. Buy a ready-made salad, or keep your supplies in the refrigerator. Advance planning and shopping will be necessary. Compile a list of "good choice" fast foods for your convenience. My list includes Wendy's® salads and Wendy's® chili (beware the sodium content, though).

○ If you are seduced by a new electronic gadget, consider whether you are about to purchase a tool or a toy. Do you **need** it to get on in life, or do you **want** it to comfort yourself?

○ If your family has a tradition of spending too much money on holiday gifts, make suggestions on ways to stick within a comfortable budget. Choose someone in your family who is probably going to be sympathetic to your viewpoint and get feedback on your suggestions first. If this person expresses agreement, ask for support.

○ If your neighbors (you know, the Joneses) buy something, that does not mean that you must make a similar acquisition.

Remember to enter new ideas and insights into your journal and remember the words of weight loss guru who has made millions:

"Change your focus, change your future."

Oprah Winfrey

Becoming an Individual Again

Exercise 1.3: Strengths and Weaknesses (20 minutes)

We each have strengths and weaknesses.

Make a list of your strengths and weaknesses in your journal and keep adding to it every time you think of something else.

For example:

○ My husband can take one bite of chocolate and put the rest away for later. Not me. If I get the taste of sugar on my tongue, I can keep going until I feel sick. It's not because he is more disciplined, it's because he is made differently. The same patterns have shown up in our children — our older son is satisfied with a modest amount of sugar, but our younger son is like me — can't stop himself once he gets started.

○ A friend of mine considers ads or commercials tempting him with a 30% savings as another way of saying that he can lose 70%.

To implement strategy, you need to draw upon your strengths and set up your lifestyle to protect yourself from your weaknesses. We all know not to buy bags of chips and Oreo cookies because, once they're in the house, they call us from deep inside the closet. But does that stop us? No. We buy them for the kids and then eat them ourselves. How much money would you save per month if you didn't buy any chips, soda, cookies or candy?

Remember to be realistic. We keep promising ourselves to go on a diet on Monday, or to get working on our household budget at the beginning of next month. But when Monday (or next month) comes, we find that all the patterns are still in place and we fall back on the very habits that we wanted to change. Systematic change is more likely to yield results than promises to turn over a new leaf.

All you're wanting to establish with this step is the bigger context in which your weight gain or money loss has occurred — and conversely, establish the bigger context in which your weight loss and financial gain can occur. As you go through the program, you will systematically integrate the elements of your choice.

Action Notes

2 what's your story?

"We are what we repeatedly do."

Aristotle

We have all come to understand, though not necessarily accept, that our weight is genetically and constitutionally influenced. In addition, for better or for worse, the eating patterns in our family of origin set in motion a lifetime relationship with food and nutrition.

Our relationship with money has been similarly formed, originating directly and indirectly from our parents — what they have taught us, what we have inherited through them (from our ancestors) and how we have reacted.

The best way to understand what we are saying is to see how this has worked in your life.

This chapter will help you explore the following layers of the behavioral bridge:

@ Genetics and Family Patterns

@ Comfort-Seeking

@ Loss of Control

@ Money = Love and Food = Love.

Remember that Comfort-Seeking includes self-medication, bingeing and addictions and Loss of Control includes lack of self-discipline and disrupted energy.

You have probably heard claims that every physical being has an electro-magnetic field, called the aura, which emanates from and surrounds the physical body. Even if you don't "believe" in the existence of auras, and would prefer a different model to explain the way we function, you will find the following information helpful.

To understand the aura, a computer system provides a useful analogy. The computer, the hardware, is analogous to your physical body — designed with certain abilities and a certain capacity. To work, the computer has to be loaded with software programs. The aura is to the physical body what software is to the computer. The software programs come from our genetics and our environment (parents, teachers and peers) during our formative years. As we go through life, our experiences become the data entered into the software programs. The programs determine how the data will be organized and used.

If you enjoy the computer software/aura analogy, we encourage you to explore the possibilities, but do remember that analogies are not facts, they are (limited) devices to assist understanding.

Important points to understand:

○ The computer can only organize data and yield the desired information if the software has been loaded. Your computer can't do word-processing without a word-processing program.

Here is a human example: if a baby doesn't receive unconditional love from his mother, the "unconditional love" program is not loaded into his aura and so unconditional love experiences cannot be entered into his aura in a systematic, usable form.

○ The computer, no matter what its design is capable of, can only function in terms of what is has, not in terms of what it does not have. All data has to be used in terms of the existing functions following the patterns determined by the programs — not the patterns *possible* in terms of the *design*.

For example, a child with musical talent can only learn to play the piano if a piano and piano lessons are provided. The talent cannot be developed in the absence of an instrument and appropriate education. However, if the child doesn't have a piano, he may learn to express the innate talent by using what is available, say using a knife and fork to tap out rhythms on the dining room table.

○ Once the program and data are in place, the computer will run along these established pathways, always yielding the same kind of results. Only an active addition of software or data, or a deletion of software or data can produce a different result.

For example, an adult can choose to change his life by training in another career (adding more software) or going for therapy to re-understand his childhood (reorganizing the data).

○ A bolt of lightning can stop a computer from functioning. Trauma or shock (physical and/or emotional) can disrupt the functioning of a living being.

For example, a person involved in a car accident might lose her memory. Usually the damage is partial and can be undetected.

Let's apply the analogy to a real life example:

A gifted child enters a piano competition for the first time. She has practiced for many months and has high hopes. She loses in the semi-finals. She is terribly upset and bursts into tears. "Never mind," says her mother, "here's a chocolate. Let's go shopping and buy you that video game you wanted." The mother means well and wants to comfort her daughter, but is unwittingly entering the following data:

○ Losing, after months of practice, doesn't need to be processed

○ Disappointment and tears are painful emotions and should be banished as quickly as possible

○ "Bad" emotions can be chased away with food, especially chocolate

○ Shopping for what you want/spending money can ease your pain

○ Now that you've experienced pain, you can get what you want

Comparison of Computer and Human	
Computer	**Human**
Hardware *has design determining capacities*	Physical Body *has design determining capacities*
Software *has to be loaded*	Aura *loaded through genetics and learning*
Appropriate Program *for desired application* *e.g. word processing for text*	Appropriate Experiences during formative years *e.g. experiencing love*
Incorrect Program *for desired application* *e.g. word processing for math*	Harmful experiences *e.g. child abuse*
No program for desired application *e.g. word processing software not loaded*	No experience *e.g. no music lessons though talented*
To Change *add software • new data • remove data and software*	To Change *add experiences • change understanding of past • new training*
Damage *bolt of lightning, virus*	Damage *trauma or shock, illness*

There are critical periods and significant moments in our lives when we are particularly susceptible to being programmed. For example, the ethologist, Konrad Lorenz demonstrated that a baby duck is designed to imprint the concept "mother" on the very first moving being that it sees when hatching from the egg. As this being is likely to be the mother duck, the system works. However, for the purposes of his study, Lorenz removed the mother duck to ensure that he would be the first being the ducklings would see when they hatched. The ducklings forever believed that Lorenz was their mother. They followed him wherever he went, as baby ducklings do, and he had to teach them to swim and fish.

You can find out how you have been "programmed," and who programmed you, by telling your story.

Discovering Your Programming

It is time to discover your personal money story, so that you can figure out what to change, what to add, what to delete and what to re-understand. For this you will need your pen and journal.

We'll lead the way, by telling our stories.

Vivien's Money Story

My father didn't go to college, but my mother did. My mother was the only mother I knew who worked. There was always a fuss if something went wrong in the house which caused expense — for example, if we needed to call the plumber. I wore hand-me-downs from my brother. I never went to the amusement park and I never asked for any money.

My brother was the opposite. When we went to restaurants, we'd be instructed to order the cheapest thing on the menu. My brother sulked, because he wanted the fancy food.

When I went to Israel on a tour, my uncle and my father gave me money. I didn't know what to do with it, so I bought a few presents and brought most of the money home and stored it under my sweaters. I didn't know how to earn money and I didn't know how to spend it.

I was rescued by two people — my uncle and my brother. My uncle was a bachelor and a lawyer. He invested money for my brother and me, and gave us money regularly. My brother had an eye for antiques and started investing when he was a teenager. Whenever he needed money, he sold the antiques at a profit. He enjoyed his material possessions, but didn't get attached to them.

My brother taught my mother how to enjoy money. I watched him carefully, and learned to spend money cautiously. I also resolved to learn to earn money, and to enjoy it, and most important of all, have enough money to pay the plumber if I needed to call one.

My mother instructed me not to be dependent on a husband for money, but to always have my own income and have a job where I could work at home, so that when I had children, I could continue to work. She also had great admiration and envy for husband and wife teams — couples who worked together. I once asked my father what his greatest fear was, and he said: "To be old and poor."

My parents were intent on paying for my education and never said "no" if I wanted to learn — even when I was already married and wanted to go to London to finish my Alexander training.

Vivien's Money Story continued

When I got my first real job, as a secretary, and I told my dad how much my (pleasing) salary was, he said: "Of course, that's nothing compared to what you're worth." That made a big impression on me. Once I certified as an Alexander teacher, my income went up rapidly, every year, and has continued to do so, ever since.

In that process, I have learned that money is elastic and immeasurable. When I earn more, I seem to have less, and when I earn less, I seem to have more. I have discovered that the reason is that when I'm earning more, I'm stressed and don't have the time to manage my money, whereas when I'm earning less, I also spend less and manage my money better.

One of our biggest difficulties since coming to this country has been shifting our understanding of money. For example, in South Africa, your mortgage rate is not fixed and interest rates are extremely high — it is therefore most desirable to pay off your mortgage — but not here in the States, where it might be better to invest the savings.

In the last year, I've discovered that, in the West, money is the route to spirituality. In order to live spiritual lives, we need to solve our personal money riddle. The answer is different for everyone. I just want to have enough money to be financially independent in my sixties, be able to travel, send my boys to college, get continuing education two to four times per year and enjoy decent, regular vacations.

I don't expect to stop working, because my work is my interest and my life's journey. My husband and I decided to work with a financial planner to reach these goals and now feel this is possible, if we stick to our plan. This gives me peace of mind, and frees me to pay attention to my quality of life and work.

Drew's Money Story

I grew up the second of three boys in a middle class family. As children, we did not receive allowances.

My first concept of money was the dollar bills I occasionally received in birthday cards from relatives. This money was mine, but clearly etched in my mind was the idea that I could not spend it all on the frivolities of youth. Some should be saved "for the future" — whatever that meant.

My first personal experience with the value of money came on a day I was with my father, in a local department store. A large plastic bag of small figures of astronauts caught my eye. I mentioned to my father how much I liked the look of the astronauts. He must have sensed that these spacemen were important to me. He asked me if I had the money at home, to pay him back, if he bought them for me.

As I remember, the space figures cost $1.88. I calculated that, even with the loss of two of my prized pieces of paper, I would have some left over for the "future." This is when money assumed a numeric value for me. I bought the spacemen and repaid my father.

I acquired my first job at eight years old. My older brother had a paper route and, when he was unable to deliver for any reason, I would substitute for him. I eventually took over the route.

With the paper route and some grass-cutting jobs, I didn't have to wait for birthdays to increase my collection of dollars. A savings account was opened for me. Savings accounts were known back then as "passbook" accounts, because you were given a small book into which your account balance was written. When you made a deposit, the teller updated the passbook and you received immediate gratification that your savings had grown. As a special treat, once a quarter, the teller would add the accrued interest to your balance. Money for nothing, I thought!

Just before I turned sixteen, my family moved to an area of town too distant to allow me to continue to service the paper route. I gave it up — and with it my ability to earn money. I was unemployed.

My father suggested that I speak to a local merchant he knew. I went downtown and asked the merchant if any jobs were available. He said that he would keep me in mind.

Several weeks later, the store called about a job — Maintenance Technician. Even with my love for words, I could not decipher that job description. A week later, I began my job at the store — as janitor.

Drew's Money Story continued

It was here that I learned about the secrecy associated with money. One day I was informed that I had been given a raise. I knew that this required a show of my appreciation to the store manager. I spotted him talking to some sales clerks. I waited my chance and thanked him. His face immediately screwed up in the most awful fashion and he looked as if he hoped the floor would open up and swallow him. He blurted out "Shhhh. Not here!" I was so embarrassed that it was a long time before I could think of the raise as a positive event. Lesson: Money is a private matter.

I entered the United States Air Force Academy after high school. This part of my life was short-lived. I made a decision to resign from the Academy. I learned about another dark side of money — guilt. The value of the USAFA education and subsequent training was estimated at well over $250,000, at the time.

I started taking courses at Ohio State University, using student loans to pay for school. I graduated with a degree in Computer Science. I got a job at a small, regional bank. Financial institutions are not well known for generously compensating their employees with cash. However, this bank offered stock options. These options allowed employees to purchase the bank's stock, in the future, for the price that the stock was at when the options were awarded. I was the recipient of quite a few of these options over the years.

One day, my boss announced that he was retiring — at age 42. He explained to me that this was possible because of his stock options. The next day I pulled out my stock option paperwork to do some calculations of my own. I saw that, if the momentum of the bank's stock price continued in two years, I would be in a situation of not ever having to work again if I maintained my moderate lifestyle. Two years and one month later, at the age of 41, I turned in my resignation.

When I retired, I was able to purchase shares of stock that were worth $60.00 on the current market for as little as $2.50! Lesson: The time value of money is incredible!

Discovering Your Money Program

One week to uncover your money program

Read through all the exercises before beginning. You will need approximately three hours of writing time. Here is a recommended daily approach to doing these exercises over a one week period.

Journaling Guide

Day 1
   Exercise 2.1

Day 2
   Exercise 2.2
   4 choices from. 2.3
   1 fast write from 2.4

Day 3
   4 choices from 2.3
   1 fast write from 2.4
   Exercise 2.5
   Begin reflection on. 2.6

Day 4
   4 choices from 2.3
   1 fast write from. 2.4
   Exercise 2.6

Day 5
   4 choices from 2.3
   1 fast write from 2.4
   Exercise 2.7

Day 6
   4 choices from 2.3
   1 fast-write from 2.4

Day 7
   4 choices from 2.3
   1 fast-write from 2.4
   Exercise 2.8
   Review of what you
   have written

As you journal, remember that you are looking for the origins and formation of these elements of the behavioral bridge:

@ Genetics and family patterns

@ Comfort-Seeking

@ Loss of Control

@ Money = Love, and Food = Love.

Your Money Program

Exercise 2.1: Fast-write Your Money Story (60 minutes)

A fast write involves writing down whatever comes to mind — quickly — without editing or censoring. Include the following elements:

○ Your parents as money role-models

○ At least one bad role-model

○ At least one good role-model

○ Significant incidents, words or events that influenced your relationship with money

○ The money atmosphere in your home of origin

○ Your current attitude and situation with money

○ What you currently want

Your Money Program

Exercise 2.2: Interesting Money Stories (20 minutes)

Make quick notes of interesting money stories you know. This could be from yourself, or someone you know, but not from someone completely unknown to you.

Your Money Program

Exercise 2.3: Examine Your Money Issues (60 minutes)

Here are some questions to help you examine your money issues. Take time to reflect and journal your answers. This can be overwhelming for some people. Do four per day for six days.

- How do you feel about money? Is it the root of all evil or is it wonderful?

- How much money do you deserve?

- What makes a person deserving of money?

- Are you jealous of people who have money?

- How do money and love relate to each other?

- How do you feel about spending money?

- How do you feel about saving money?

- Are you able to ask people for money?

- When someone gives you money, how do you feel?

- How much money is enough?

- What's your money wish?

- Does someone owe you money?

- Is how much you earn linked to your self-esteem?

- If your earning power isn't linked to your self-esteem, what is?

- How much money do you think you should be earning?

- How do you sabotage your ability to earn?

- How do you sabotage your ability to invest?

- Can you loan money to a friend?

- Can you accept money from a friend?

- Can you give money to a relative?

- Can you accept money from a relative?

- Do you like paying for other people at restaurants, etc? Why?

- Can you let others pay for you at a restaurant?

- What's the most important shift you need to make with regard to money?

Your Money Program

Exercise 2.4: Do a Daily Fast-Write (10 minutes)

Begin with ONE of the following prompts, or any prompt of your own choice. Choose **one** per day, for six days.

○ I don't like thinking about money because ...

○ Today, I feel good about money because ...

○ I wish I had more money because then ...

○ The first thing I would do if I had enough money is ...

○ The world would be a better place without money because ...

○ I like thinking about money because ...

○ There are some things that are more important than money, such as ...

○ I have enough money, but ...

○ I would ask (name a person) for help with money, except ...

○ I wish I could relate to money the way (name a person) does, because then ...

○ The most important priority in my life is ...
   and more money could help me with this in the following way ...

Your Money Program

Exercise 2.5: Relationship with Money Profile (10 minutes)

Circle the word in each pair which better describes your relationship with money:

open	private	sharing	individual
focused	dreamy	community	personal
realistic	wishful	needy	independent
open	secretive	energized	floppy
obsessive	relaxed	sharp	diffused
aware	confused	anxious	hopeful
messy	organized	happy	sad
flush	tight	despairing	enthusiastic
generous	cautious	thrifty	spendthrift
on time	late	systematic	whatever
overdraft	savings	on edge	cushioned
compulsive	controlled	adventurous	safe
strategic	impulsive	handicapped	athletic
financial plan	no plan	empowered	dependent
knowledgeable	confused	tense	fun
precise	general	rich	poor

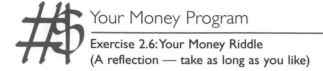 Your Money Program

Exercise 2.6: Your Money Riddle
(A reflection — take as long as you like)

A riddle is a question whose answer is camouflaged in paradox or double meaning, for example:

○ What goes up when the rain comes down? An umbrella.

○ What is black and white and red all over? The newspaper. Red = read

Here is an example: Suzy is very frustrated with her elderly mother because she worries so much about money even though she clearly has enough. The irony is that Suzy had enough money to retire in her early fifties, but continues to worry about money — just like her mother! **Suzy has been programmed that** *any thinking about money* **has to take the form of "worrying."**
Suzy's riddle: How can I think about money, but not be like my mother?

Vivien's Money Riddle

I want to be free of needing to earn money, so that I can do the work I love.
Riddle: How can I be free of money?
Answer: By having so much I don't need any more.

Drew's Money Riddle

How come something so hard for everyone else, was so easy for me?

Drew retired at the age of 41. Money did not pose a riddle for him. He went with what we all know: spend less than you earn and invest the savings. The money riddle for him, is "Where's the riddle?"

Drew also solved another huge riddle: How much is enough? Drew lives in a modest home suited to his needs and lives a lifestyle of simple abundance. If he were to decide on a more extravagant lifestyle, he might have to go back to work.

However, retiring at 41 does not solve all the riddles of life. What comes after money? We'll let Drew puzzle over his new riddle, although the answer is, of course, in the pages of this book!

Back to you: What is your personal money riddle?

Take as much time as you need on this, but keep moving forward with the program, holding the question in the back of your mind. Our money riddles are hidden from us. If you say to yourself: "I wonder what my money riddle is?" the answer will eventually appear to you.

○ What is the solution to the riddle?

The solution will be hidden inside the riddle. Again allow the answer to come to you. Be patient, but maintain the conscious desire for the solution to appear.

It can be useful to work backwards from the endpoint. If you describe to yourself how your life will look once you've solved the riddle (for example Vivien wanted to be free from money worries to fully focus on the work she loves), you will most likely be able to ascertain the substance of the riddle, if not the actual wording.

How will your life look once you have solved your money riddle?

Your Money Program

Exercise 2.7: A Conversation with Your "Self" (20 minutes)

Identify the part of yourself that has been most damaged by money.

○ What happened?

○ What can heal you?

○ What does your "self" want most from money?

○ What is your "self" unwilling to do for money?
(excluding illegal & dishonest acts)

The answer to this last question is usually very significant, revealing the very thing that will help you get your money situation straightened out.

Write the answers in your journal.

Your New Money Program

Exercise 2.8: Rewriting Your Money Story (20 minutes)

Fast write your new money story, reversing the directional flow of the undesirable aspects/limitations of your original fast write.

For example in my story, my mother programmed me to work at home and be able to work and look after my children simultaneously. In my rewritten script, I reverse that, and I'm comfortable working anywhere where my work is appreciated and I earn in accordance with my worth. I no longer have to be physically present to be taking good care of my children.

Watch out for scripting that has worked in the past, and in context, but prevents you from reaching your full potential. Be sure to include the following:

○ An improved relationship with money

○ A way of earning/having/spending enough money

○ A plan for taking yourself from your current situation to your desired situation

○ A list of resources that you're going to draw upon

○ A desired outcome

Remember that you are looking to reverse the elements of the behavioral bridge, so that you establish the opposite qualities of:

❂ Conscious Choice

❂ Contentment

❂ Control

❂ Love=Love and Money=Money

Discovering Your Weight Program

One week to uncover your weight program

It is time to discover your personal weight program, so that you can figure out what to change, what to add, what to delete and what to re-understand. For this you will need your pen and journal.

Read through all the exercises before beginning. You will need a total of three hours. Here is a recommended daily approach to doing these exercises over a one week period:

Journaling Guide

Day 1
    Exercise 2.9

Day 2
    Exercise 2.10
    4 choices from 2.11
    1 fast write from 2.12

Day 3
    4 choices from 2.11
    1 fast write from 2.12
    Exercise 2.13
    Begin reflection on 2.14

Day 4
    4 choices from 2.11
    1 fast write from 2.12
    Exercise 2.14

Day 5
    4 choices from 2.11
    1 fast write from 2.12
    Exercise 2.15

Day 6
    4 choices from 2.11
    1 fast-write from 2.12

Day 7
    4 choices from 2.11
    1 fast-write from 2.12
    Exercise 2.16
    Review of what you have written

Vivien's Weight Story

I was a skinny kid. Photographs show big knobby knees on stick-like legs. When I was ten, my hair was cut very short and I was continually mistaken for a boy. My father was very pleased with this. When people asked if I was a boy or a girl, he told them: "A boy of course." I wanted to please my father, but I was also getting to the age when I needed to enjoy the identity of being a girl.

Another line that sticks in my mind, is that my father would always admire people who were lean: "Not an ounce of fat!" he would say, and he took great care not to put on weight himself.

In contrast to this, my mother always struggled with her weight, although she was not obese. Every now and then, she would take herself in hand and put herself on a diet. I definitely did not want to be overweight and I feared that by becoming a woman this would inevitably happen.

I went on my first diet when I was thirteen, wanting to "lose" the bulge around my middle. I didn't know that the bulge was not caused by fat, but by a combination of my big rib cage and poor posture. I began the diet, but became discouraged the following weekend when my mother and I bumped into a friend of hers. "This is Vivien?" said the friend, "the one who wants to diet? Why does she want to diet?"

I did not hear: "Vivien is thin — she doesn't need to diet." I heard: "Dieting won't work for Vivien." I felt defeated. I could tell that the diet wasn't going to yield the results I wanted.

I had the usual body image problems as a teenager, but weight wasn't my big problem. I was very active and played a lot of sports. I went through a bad turn at the age of fifteen when I discovered I'd put on ten pounds, but that turned out to be caused by growing two inches. A few months lagged between trying to lose the extra weight and discovering the reason. I still think that it is telling, that what the scales said could have been so much more powerful than the mirror.

The next bad turn happened when I started using birth control pills. I immediately gained five pounds, which I couldn't lose, no matter how hard I tried. I took up long distance running and that helped me control my weight for many years. The other way I controlled my weight was through my interest in diet and nutrition.

When I was nineteen, I became interested in whole foods. I gave up all refined foods, sugar and coffee. By the time I was twenty-three I was a vegetarian. Soon after we married, my husband and I opted for a macrobiotic diet (the brown rice-based diet which balances yin and yang foods.) That lasted until I was pregnant with my second child, at the age of thirty-three.

Vivien's Weight Story continued

On a visit to London, at the age of twenty-seven, I was advised by a practitioner that I was intolerant to certain foods, including wheat and dairy. During my second pregnancy, I read a book which explained how food intolerance is passed from mother to child and I decided to stop eating all wheat, dairy and sugar, for three months. This narrowed my options so severely that I realized it was time to go back to meat and potatoes — it would not be healthy to stick rigidly to a diet with so little variety.

On the day after I gave birth, I weighed myself. Avoiding the foods that didn't agree with my body had really worked — *I was at my ideal weight!* The motivation (program) to protect my child had worked best to bring me the weight loss results I desired.

But that was the last time. After my first child was born, my weight had plummeted during the nursing phase. Now, with my second child, the hormones played an ugly trick on me and I started to gain weight, which I could not lose.

Soon after this, we moved from South Africa to the United States of America. We dropped our careful eating habits in favor of trying every possible taste sensation in the land of plenty. I put on ten pounds in six weeks.

After a few months, I got sick of feeling fat and being asked if I were pregnant again. I put myself back on a weight loss diet. I hadn't realized that a plate of food in the Midwest was a plate of food seasoned with fat! I did lose the weight, but ever since then I have been struggling against weight gain.

About six years ago I joined Weight Watchers®. At first, I was turned away because I didn't qualify. I explained that I could feel I was about to put on weight again and the counselor became more sympathetic. I did maintain my weight, but life became busy and I stopped going to meetings. Sure enough, I put on fifteen pounds. By returning to Weight Watchers® and following their program, I did manage to lose the weight and become a Lifetime Member.

The Weight Watcher® program was very good for me. I realized that I had spent my entire adult life on some kind of restricted diet — vegetarian, macrobiotic, food intolerant, detox or whatever had most recently caught my interest. I had no idea how to eat when faced with free choice, I just wanted to eat everything, because now was my chance — obviously the coming Monday meant going back onto some kind of strict regime.

Vivien's Weight Story continued

Once again, life became overwhelmingly busy and I stopped going to meetings. The pounds came back faster than I could say "Boo!" even though I was as active and fit as ever. (I have been fit my whole life, exercising, on average, 5 days per week.) The truth is, I love to eat and food is a delicious tranquilizer. There is no doubt that I eat more and make poor food choices when I am under stress.

As I write this, I am twenty pounds over the weight I "should" be. But that is better than the twenty-eight pounds of a few weeks ago when we had the weight loss, money gain insight. Yes, I'm excited to report that the program is working for me. In that moment of insight I realized that I am approaching fifty. It is time for me to accept that my body has changed and so has my metabolism.

Carbohydrates, my favorite tranquilizer, are no longer my best friends and should be eaten in very small quantities. I'm eating salads, vegetables and protein, combining all the knowledge about diet and nutrition I have learned over the years and coming up with a new solution for the person that I am now.

I have reviewed my life and I can see that it *will not be better if I am thinner.* Nobody else cares about my weight — only me. But, *my life will be better if I take care of the stress* that triggers me into eating too much. And my life will be better if I give myself time to take care of myself.

My weight is truly a symptom of the program that I'm acting out and I feel empowered knowing that I have enough training and knowledge to choose a different program. I am reprogramming myself to accept that I am a woman now, with a woman's shape, and the slender nineteen-year-old has gone forever, in more ways than one.

Drew's Weight Story

Needless to say, Drew doesn't have a weight story. He's trying to make up something now about having once needed to gain weight. Anyway, what would you expect from someone who doesn't have a money riddle? Further proof that the weight and money issues go together.

Your Weight Program

Exercise 2.9: Fast-write Your Weight Story (60 minutes)

A fast write involves writing down whatever comes to mind — quickly — without editing or censoring. Leave spaces for extra notes later. Include the following elements:

○ Your parents' relationships with their weight

○ When and how you first "realized" that you should lose weight

○ At least one bad diet role-model

○ At least one good diet role-model

○ Significant incidents, words or events that influenced your relationship with food, eating, diet and body image

○ The atmosphere in your home of origin around meal times, using food to celebrate or as treats, issues with weight

○ Your current attitude toward your weight, dieting and body image

○ What you currently desire for yourself regarding weight, diet and body image

Remember that you are looking for the origins and formation of these elements of the behavioral bridge:

@ Genetics and Family Patterns

@ Comfort-Seeking

@ Loss of Control

@ Money = Love and Food = Love

Your Weight Program

Exercise 2.10: Interesting Weight Stories (20 minutes)

Make quick notes of interesting weight stories you know. This could be from yourself, or someone you know, but not from someone completely unknown to you.

Your Weight Program

Exercise 2.11: Examine Your Weight Issues (60 minutes)

Here are some questions to help you examine your weight issues.
Take time to reflect and journal your answers.

- How do you feel about weight? Are thin people better than fat people?

- How much should you weigh?

- Should you be punished if you aren't the "right" weight?

- What makes a person the "right" weight?

- Are you jealous of people who are thinner than you?
  Can eat whatever they want?

- How do you relate food and love?

- Do thin people deserve more fun than fat people?

- What is more important, health or looks?

- Is eating a form of self-destruction? Are you putting your life at risk?

- Is your weight linked to your self-esteem?

- What else about your life will change if you lose weight?

- If your weight isn't linked to your self-esteem, what is?

- How do you sabotage your ability to lose weight?

- What's the most important shift you need to make
  with regard to weight loss?

- Are you seeking someone else's approval through weight loss?

- Who can support you in your desire to lose weight?

Your Weight Program

Exercise 2.12: For one week, Do a Daily Fast-Write

Beginning with one of the following prompts, or any prompt of your own choice. Choose one per day:

○ I don't like thinking about my weight because ...

○ Today, I feel good about my weight because ...

○ I wish I weighed less because then ...

○ The first thing I would do if I were the right weight is ...

○ The world would be a better place if we all weighed the right amount because ...

○ I like thinking about weight because ...

○ There are some things that are more important than my weight, such as ...

○ My weight doesn't matter, but ...

○ I would ask (name a person) for help, except ...

○ I wish I could relate to my weight the way (name a person) does, because then ...

○ The most important priority in my life is ... and being the right weight could help me with this in the following way ...

Your Weight Program

Exercise 2.13: Relationship with Weight Profile (10 minutes)

Circle the word in each pair which better describes your relationship with weight:

open	private		rigid	loose
focused	dreamy		faddish	individual
realistic	wishful		energized	floppy
open	secretive		sharp	diffused
obsessive	relaxed		anxious	hopeful
aware	confused		happy	sad
haphazard	organized		despairing	enthusiastic
greedy	restrictive		systematic	whatever
compulsive	controlled		handicapped	athletic
strategic	impulsive		empowered	dependent
knowledgeable	confused		tense	fun
disciplined	emotional		scientific	fashionable

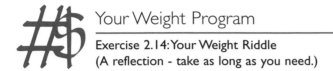

Your Weight Program

Exercise 2.14: Your Weight Riddle
(A reflection - take as long as you need.)

What is your personal weight riddle?*

What is the solution?

How will your life look once you have solved your weight riddle?

* A riddle is a question whose answer is camouflaged in paradox or double meaning — e.g. what goes up when the rain comes down? An umbrella. What is black and white and red all over? The newspaper. Red = read

---

Vivien's Weight Riddle

Actually, I have two:

1. How can I please my father if I look like a woman?

   Solution: That's an old tape from my childhood. By this time, my father accepts that I'm a woman. Now it's my turn. I have to learn to please myself by looking like a woman.

2. How can I take care of my weight without being obsessed?

   Solution: Pay attention to the lifestyle triggers that cause weight gain, not the weight itself.

Your Weight Program

Exercise 2.15: Conversation with Your "Self" (20 minutes)

Identify the part of yourself that has been most damaged by your weight program. Journal the answers to these questions.

○ What happened?

○ What can heal you?

○ What does your "self" want most in regard to your weight?

○ What is your "self" unwilling to do for the "right weight?"

Your New Weight Program

Exercise 2.16: Rewriting Your Weight Story (20 minutes)

Fast write your new weight story, giving yourself power to deal with the undesirable aspects/limitations of you original fast write.

For example, if you have not been the right weight since the age of 19, your rewrite would include a realization that that is not the right weight for you now and a framing of how you can successfully reach what is the right weight for you now.

Watch out for scripting that has worked in the past, and in context, but prevents you from reaching your full potential. For example: do not prescribe for yourself the exercise routine that helped you lose weight twenty years ago — that may no longer be applicable at this stage of your life.

Be sure to include the following:

○ An improved relationship with your weight

○ A way of being the "right" weight

○ A plan for taking yourself from your current situation to your desired situation

○ A list of resources that you're going to draw upon

○ A desired outcome

Remember that you are looking to reverse the elements of the behavioral bridge, so that you establish the opposite qualities of:

◉ Conscious Choice

◉ Contentment

◉ Control

◉ Love = Love and Food = Food

45

Action Notes

3
where are you?

Excessive Consumption • Imbalance • Loss of Control • Comfort Seeking • Genetics and Family Patterns • Environmental Influences • Money = Love and Food = Love

> "Start where you are,
> do what you can."
>
> Arthur Ashe

Well, you've discovered your programs. What have your programs yielded? Now for the cold, hard facts — the actual numbers. This chapter will help you assess your status with regard to:

@ Excessive consumption

@ Imbalance between what's coming in and what's going out

Please don't judge yourself. Self acceptance is an important initial step to change.

If you found yourself in Los Angeles, California and a stranger asked you how he could get to San Francisco, you would have the ability to help him. Since you would know where you are (Los Angeles) and you know that Interstate Route 5 connects San Francisco and Los Angeles, you could advise the stranger to take I-5 for his journey.

This information is necessary, but not sufficient. You have indicated to the stranger that the highway he must use is I-5, but you haven't given him the **direction** in which to travel the highway. If he finds I-5 and travels South instead of North, he will probably be at least mildly upset to find that he ended up in San Diego, instead of San Francisco. Oh well, he was just a stranger anyway. What do you care about his direction?

But, would you care about **your direction** on the same highway? Well, if the starting point city (in this example, Los Angeles) represents your current situation, San Francisco represents your future goals, and the path (I-5) is the method by which you will attain your goals, you must recognize the importance of direction.

We will cover **direction** in a bit. Right now, we want to discover your **starting place**. This place represents what your money-related and weight-related software and data have yielded up to this point in your life.

Establishing Where You Are — Money

Before you take any trip, you need to know where you are. We are preparing for a trip, so let's find out where your starting place is.

Net Worth Calculation

This is the portion of our program where we will start looking at some numbers. DO NOT PANIC! I will not subject you to wading through endless financial formulas. I have spent a great deal of my life dealing with numbers in a variety of settings. I have learned that the vast majority of people do not share my love of math and all of its eccentricities. I respect that and will enable you to get the most out of the financial side of this program without having to deal with the underlying theories and computational minutia.

In fact, I will make you a promise. I will show you only **one** mathematical formula in this whole program. Just one. Even better, you will only be asked to do calculations using formulas if you want to, because we will be providing you with Quick Charts.

Take a look at the "Net Worth Worksheet" on page 52.

Read through all the instructions in exercise 3.1 and then just fill in the blanks on the worksheet.

Helpful hint: If you have recently applied for a mortgage loan, you probably had to come up with these numbers for that document. Your financial institution will have given you a copy of this information when you closed on your loan. Take the information, update it to reflect your current standing and enter the data in the appropriate section of the worksheet. [By the way, if you found these figures difficult to locate, now is a **great** time to start a financial information filing system. Get some folders, label them and start using them to keep track of your financial records.]

Establishing Where You Are — Money

Exercise 3.1: Net Worth Calculation (30 minutes)
Use the Worksheet on page 52

○ On the left side of the "Net Worth" Worksheet, detail all of your money-based assets. These are checking/savings account balances, certificates of deposit, stocks, bonds — you get the idea. The "Other" categories are included on the worksheet in case you have some assets that most people generally do not (e.g. ownership shares in a private company, assets in a partnership, etc.)

○ I generally advise people not to include houses and automobiles on this list. They are most definitely assets, but they are very illiquid (you are not likely to sell your house, take the money and not buy a new one) and will unnecessarily skew your net worth calculation figures. [Technically, this reduces your Net Worth Worksheet into your "Working" Net Worth Worksheet. This is a very minor difference. We will continue to refer to it simply as your Net Worth Worksheet.]

○ On the right side of the worksheet, detail your money-based liabilities. These are credit card balances, personal loans, store charge cards, and student loans — anything you owe to someone else. Use the "Other" entries if you can think of a liability you have that is in a category that I missed (any place where you have borrowed money). I've asked you to leave out your home and automobiles as assets on the left side so don't include your mortgage loan and car loan balances on the right as liabilities.

○ Total each of the two columns.

○ Subtract the right total from the left total. This is your current **net worth**.

Exercise 3.1 CONTINUED

Net Worth Worksheet #1				
Assets			**Liabilities**	
Item	Amount		Item	Amount
Checking Accounts			Personal Loans	
Savings Accounts			Student Loans	
Stocks			Credit Cards	
Bonds			Other	
Certificates of Deposit			Other	
Mutual Funds			Other	
Retirement Accounts			Total	
Other			**Net Worth Calculation**	
Other			Asset Total - Liability Total = Net Worth	
Other				
Total				

Well, you found out where you are. The Net Worth Rating chart below shows all the possible outcomes.

Net Worth Rating		
Assets - Liabilities	**Outcome**	**Comment**
Negative	You are starting out in a less-than-favorable place	*Don't Panic!*
Zero	Your starting place is neutral	*Nice!*
Positive	You are starting out great	*Don't Get Cocky Yet!*

Does your net worth total have a negative sign in front of it? Not to worry. Depending upon where you are in your money life, this is not necessarily a concern. If the **direction** of your financial journey is good (which we will discover soon), time will soon turn that negative into a positive. If your net worth is zero or a positive number, your next goal will be to make it a positive number or a larger positive number.

Regardless, you are in much better shape knowing where you are, than having no idea.

That's it for now. You have completed one of the few "number crunching" chores that will be asked of you in this program. Was that so bad?

Establishing Where You Are — Weight

Exercise 3.2: Weight, Size, Physical Condition and Eating Patterns (20 minutes)

This takes even less time than establishing where you are financially, but may be a little more painful (or not). Enter the following information in your journal:

_____ Your Current Weight

_____ Your Clothes Size

Circle the word which best describes your physical condition. This is a reflection of how you feel about yourself. Only a consultation with a qualified fitness consultant can give you an accurate reading.

○ Cardio-vascular fitness   Poor   Fair   Good

○ Strength   Poor   Fair   Good

○ Flexibility   Poor   Fair   Good

Exercise 3.2 CONTINUED

Other items to "weigh-in":

How can you change the following patterns to support a new lifestyle? Do a five minute daily reflection on this in your journal for seven days.

○ How do your grocery shopping patterns replicate learning from your childhood?

○ How do your eating out patterns replicate learning from childhood?

○ Do you use food as a reward?

○ Do you have family meal times? What is the atmosphere?

○ Do you snack while you watch TV?

○ Do you cat between meals?

○ Do you eat healthy meals but unhealthy snacks?

○ How frequently do you eat fast foods?

○ How frequently do you eat in restaurants?

Rate the nutritional and health qualities of your meals:

     Poor   Fair   Good   Excellent

Action Notes

4 are you headed?

Excessive Consumption • Imbalance • Loss of Control / Comfort Seeking • Genetics and Family Patterns • Environmental Influences • Love and Food = Love • Money = Love

"If you don't know
   where you want to go,
then it doesn't matter
   where you end up."

Will Rogers

In chapter 3, we determined the starting point of your journey and we encouraged you not to be too concerned about that starting point.

Remember, **where you are** currently is less important than **where you are going** — your direction.

This chapter will help you establish your direction and reveal the extent of the —

@ Imbalance between what is coming in and what is going out.

Calculating your Financial Direction

Remember that I warned you not to celebrate yet if your net worth is positive? That is because you can begin with a positive net worth, be saving money and still be heading in the wrong direction. You could also begin with a negative net worth but be heading in the right direction. We will show you that there are **nine possible outcomes** when you combine net worth with your monthly income and expenses.

But, we haven't yet worked out your monthly income and expenses. First, I want to motivate you by demonstrating the significance of the information that you will soon provide for yourself.

Take a glance at the worksheets, starting on page 60.

These worksheets represent a portion of Ann Smith's financial journey. Notice that there are two sets of Ann's Net Worth Worksheets — one for January and one for February. We need to compare the two Net Worth Worksheets, to determine the direction of Ann's journey.

Ann is single and 34 years old. She still has to finish paying off her tuition loan. She has some modest investments. She rents an apartment and just bought a new car. Take a look at her worksheets on the following pages.

Ann Smith - January - Net Worth Worksheet

Assets		Liabilities	
Item	Amount	Item	Amount
Checking Accounts	$100.00	Personal Loans	$0.00
Savings Accounts	500.00	Student Loans	5,000.00
Stocks	0.00	Credit Cards	2,500.00
Bonds	500.00	Other	0.00
Certificates of Deposit	2,000.00	Other	0.00
Mutual Funds	1,500.00	Other	0.00
Retirement Accounts	0.00	Total	$7,500.00
Other	0.00	**Net Worth Calculation**	
Other	0.00	Asset Total - Liability Total = Net Worth	
Other	0.00	$4,100.00 - $7,500.00 = -$3,400.00	
Total	$4,100.00	(Total Net Worth)	

Ann Smith - Income Worksheet

Item	Amount	Item	Amount
Personal Income	$2,400.00	Rental Income	$0.00
Alimony	0.00	Stock Dividends	0.00
Child Support	0.00	Other	0.00
		Total Income	$2,400.00

Ann Smith - Expense Worksheet

Item	Amount	Item	Amount
Mortgage/Rent	$750.00	Day Care/Babysitting	$0.00
Alimony	0.00	Club/Organization Dues	50.00
Child Support	0.00	Medical/Health Insurance	125.00
Automobile Payments	350.00	Prescriptions	10.00
Credit Card Payments	50.00	Children's Tuition	0.00
Equity Line Payments	0.00	Course Tuition (personal)	15.00
Personal Loan payments	0.00	Haircuts	50.00
Student Loan payments	125.00	Church Tithing	20.00
Bank fees	0.00	Vet Expenses	0.00
Restaurants	150.00	Real Estate Taxes	0.00
Entertainment	50.00	Gifts/Presents	50.00
Hobbies/interests	50.00	Vacation	60.00
Electric	50.00	Children's Clothing	0.00
Gas - home	0.00	Personal Clothing	100.00
Water	0.00	Dental Visits	10.00
Home Telephone	25.00	Doctor Visits	5.00
Cell phone	35.00	Auto Insurance	65.00
Long Distance	24.00	Home Insurance	0.00
Internet fees	50.00	Charitable Contributions	25.00
Gas - auto	75.00	Home Repair/Maintenance	0.00
Cable TV	80.00	Subscriptions	0.00
Newspaper	15.00	Auto licenses	6.00
Groceries	200.00	Tax Prep./Accountant	0.00
Children's Allowance	0.00	Legal fees	0.00
House Cleaning	0.00	Safe deposit box fees	0.00
Lawn Care	0.00	Miscellaneous	150.00
Dry Cleaning	0.00	Expense Total	$2,800.00

Income (from pg. 60) $2,400.00 - Expenses $2,800 = -$400.00

Ann Smith - February - Net Worth Worksheet				
Assets		**Liabilities**		
Item	Amount	Item	Amount	
Checking Accounts	$100.00	Personal Loans	$0.00	
Savings Accounts	500.00	Student Loans	4,875.00	
Stocks	0.00	Credit Cards	2,850.00	
Bonds	500.00	Other	0.00	
Certificates of Deposit	2,000.00	Other	0.00	
Mutual Funds	1,500.00	Other	0.00	
Retirement Accounts	0.00	Total	$7,725.00	
Other	0.00	**Net Worth Calculation**		
Other	0.00	Asset Total - Liability Total = Net Worth		
Other	0.00	$4,100.00 - $7,725.00 = -$3,6250.00		
Total	4,100.00	(Total Net Worth)		

Note: Ann's net worth has decreased even though her income & expense remains the same.

Look at Ann's January Net Worth Worksheet. Her net worth was negative at the time she completed the worksheet (-$3,400 to be exact). So we have established Ann's starting position on her financial journey. It's not the best — but let's see in which direction she is headed.

Turn your attention to Ann's Income and Expense Worksheets.

○ Her total monthly expenses ($2,800.00) are $400 greater than her total monthly income ($2,400.00), so the calculation of her income minus her expenses yields a -$400.00.

○ She is in a deficit spending situation. At the end of the month, she has no money to add an asset or reduce a liability.

○ Since she spends more than she earns, the $400.00 must be added to one of her liabilities or subtracted from one of her assets.

The $400 difference does not translate dollar for dollar into a $400 difference in her net worth the following month. Here's why:

Remember that she did reduce some of her outstanding debts by paying on the loans ($125.00 on her student loan and $50.00 on her credit card balance).

Look at the net effect on these two loans on her February Net Worth Worksheet.

These liabilities were reduced, but Ann's monthly spending still outpaces her income by $400.00. The money has to come from somewhere. So, Ann chooses to make up her deficit by charging more to her credit cards:

Now the credit card balance math looks like this: ———————→

These new balances were entered into her February Net Worth Worksheet and it was re-tallied. Take a look at the result. Compare the balance of her student loan entry in January to the February number. Do you see how it reflects the payment made?

Do the same with her credit card entries. It is imperative that this point makes sense to you! If it doesn't, you must re-read this until you fully understand, or you will continue to spiral down in debt.

**Ann Smith
Effect of Student Loan Payment**

Starting Balance	$5,000.00
January Payment	- $125.00
New Balance	$4,875.00

**Ann Smith
Effect of Credit Card Payment**

Starting Balance	$2,500.00
January Payment	- $50.00
New Balance	$2,450.00

**Ann Smith
Income Deficit On Credit Card**

Starting Balance	$2,500.00
January Payment	- $50.00
New Balance	$2,450.00
Additional Charges	$400.00
Corrected Balance	$2,850.00

By the way, you might notice that I have not included loan and credit card interest charges at this point. This was merely for the sake of not cluttering up the calculations and worksheet entries. It in no way signifies that I think those monthly interest charges are unimportant — just the opposite. This topic will be dealt with when we discuss compound interest later.

○ Now look at the big picture. Compare Ann's total net worth number from January, -$3,400, to the same figure in February, -$3,625. Do you see that it has gotten even lower?

Ann's Net Worth Comparison Worksheet

Net Worth Total (February)	-$3,625.00
— Net Worth Total (January)	- -$3,400.00
Monthly Change in Net Worth	-$225.00

Final result: Ann's net worth gets more negative with every subsequent month. February is $225 worse than January (-$3,625.00) — March will be $225 worse than February (-$3,850.00), etc. At the end of two years, Ann's net worth will be -$8,800.00.

Where Ann started is irrelevant — she is headed in the wrong direction.

Ann's Future Net Worth Comparison Worksheet

Monthly Change in Net Worth		-$225.00
Multiply by 24 (months)	x	24
Result		- $5,400.00
(Add) Net Worth from January	+	-$3,400.00
Future Net Worth in 2 Years		-$8,800.00

What about the opposite situation? What happens if you start out in a good position, but head the wrong way? That is the case with Mary. I think we should take a break from worksheets, so we will just chat about Mary's situation.

Mary's starting point (her January net worth figure) was $15,000. Nice start. The beginning of Mary's financial journey is at a better place.

At one time, she must have had a handle on the right direction. However, now she finds herself changing direction for the worse. Her current monthly expenses are $300 more than her income. If she continues on this tack, she will eventually eat away her positive net worth and be in an unfavorable position. Favorable starting place; unfavorable direction.

Mike's case illustrates the situation where nothing is happening. He starts out well enough (net worth at $3,000), but the difference between his income and expenses is zero. His situation doesn't get any worse from month to month, but it doesn't get any better either. Mike is treading water. Favorable starting place; no direction. Mike will really have to motivate himself to plan his financial future.

Well we've looked at a financial journey that starts out less than favorable and gets worse, one that starts out favorably but gets worse and one where nothing is happening.

There is one more that we should mention. Here is an example where the starting place is negative, but the direction is positive:

Tom and Mary Martin are in quite a different situation than Ann. They are married and they both work. They have two small children. Since their household situation is much different than Ann's, you would expect their financial situation to be different as well. And it is. Review their worksheets on the following pages and then we will compare their situation to Ann's in a little more depth, as we map out their financial journey.

"Ultimately, we know deeply
that the other side of every fear is freedom."
Marilyn Ferguson

The Martins - January - Net Worth Worksheet

Assets			Liabilities	
Item	**Amount**		**Item**	**Amount**
Checking Accounts	$500.00		Personal Loans	$1,400.00
Savings Accounts	2000.00		Student Loans	2,000.00
Stocks	1,500.00		Credit Cards	2,000.00
Bonds	0.00		Equity Line	8,000.00
Certificates of Deposit	500.00		Other	0.00
Mutual Funds	1,000.00		Other	0.00
Retirement Accounts	2,500.00		Total	$13,400.00
Other	0.00			
Other	0.00			
Other	0.00			
Total	$8,000.00			

Net Worth Calculation

Asset Total - Liability Total = Net Worth

$8,000.00 - $13,400.00 = -$5,400.00
(Total Net Worth)

The Martins - Income Worksheet

Item	Amount		Item	Amount
Personal Income	$6,865.00		Rental Income	$0.00
Alimony	0.00		Stock Dividends	35.00
Child Support	0.00		Other	0.00
			Total Income	$6,900.00

The Martins - Expense Worksheet

Item	Amount	Item	Amount
Mortgage/Rent	$1,300.00	Day Care/Babysitting	$300.00
Alimony	0.00	Club/Organization Dues	50.00
Child Support	0.00	Medical/Health Insurance	125.00
Automobile Payments	800.00	Prescriptions	10.00
Credit Card Payments	200.00	Children's Tuition	0.00
Equity Line Payments	500.00	Course Tuition (personal)	23.00
Personal Loan Payments	100.00	Haircuts	75.00
Student Loan Payments	100.00	Church Tithing	45.00
Bank Fees	15.00	Vet Expenses	0.00
Restaurants	100.00	Real Estate Taxes	300.00
Entertainment	50.00	Gifts/Presents	50.00
Hobbies/interests	55.00	Vacation	145.00
Electric	125.00	Children's Clothing	71.00
Gas - Home	50.00	Personal Clothing	150.00
Water	30.00	Dental Visits	20.00
Home Telephone	25.00	Doctor Visits	25.00
Cell phone	60.00	Auto Insurance	98.00
Long Distance	30.00	Home Insurance	72.00
Internet fees	50.00	Charitable Contributions	50.00
Gas - Auto	200.00	Home Repair/Maintenance	85.00
Cable TV	100.00	Subscriptions	10.00
Newspaper	20.00	Auto Licenses	9.00
Groceries	400.00	Tax Prep./Accountant	0.00
Children's Allowance	25.00	Legal fees	0.00
House Cleaning	0.00	Safe deposit box fees	2.00
Lawn Care	0.00	Miscellaneous	400.00
Dry Cleaning	50.00	Expense Total	$6,500

Income (from pg. 66) $6,900.00 - Expenses $6,500 = $400.00

The Martins - February - Net Worth Worksheet

Assets			Liabilities		
Item	Amount		Item	Amount	
Checking Accounts	$900.00		Personal Loans	$1,200.00	
Savings Accounts	2000.00		Student Loans	1,900.00	
Stocks	1,500.00		Credit Cards	1,900.00	
Bonds	0.00		Equity Line	7,500.00	
Certificates of Deposit	500.00		Other	0.00	
Mutual Funds	1,000.00		Other	0.00	
Retirement Accounts	2,500.00		Total	$12,500.00	
Other	0.00		**Net Worth Calculation**		
Other	0.00		Asset Total - Liability Total = Net Worth		
Other	0.00		$8,400.00 - $12,500.00 = -$4,100.00		
Total	$8,400.00		(Total Net Worth)		

We will now explore the Martins' financial situation just like we did Ann's. Start at their starting place — January's Net Worth Worksheet. Looks like they start out in a place worse than Ann. Their net worth is -$5,400 versus Ann's -$3,400. At first glance you might wish you were Ann rather than the Martins.

But wait a minute. Didn't I tell you that direction was more important than starting place when it comes to your overall financial journey?

The Martins' Income and Expense Worksheets show that they spend $400 less per month than they earn ($6,500 vs. $6,900).

What will this difference mean to them over time?

On their February Net Worth Worksheet, all of their liability entries have been reduced by the corresponding payment amounts in their January Expense Worksheet (Personal loans by $200, Student loans by $100, etc.).

The Martin's Net Worth Comparison Worksheet	
Net Worth Total (February)	– $4,100.00
— Net Worth Total (January)	– –$5,400.00
Monthly Change in Net Worth	$1,300.00

Those payments by themselves certainly had an effect on their total net worth figure. But, the Martins get a bonus! Because they spend less than they earn on a monthly basis, they have money left over which can be applied to their net worth.

Just as Ann had to account for her $400 monthly deficit by adding it to her credit card balance, the Martins have to account for their extra $400. They decided to put the money in their checking account (whose balance has increased from $500 to $900). They could have used the extra $400 to reduce one of their liabilities (like paying more on one of their loans). The net effect on their total net worth would have been the same.

All told, the Martins are now $1,300 better off. Their total net worth went from -$5,400 to -$4,100.

If they keep traveling in this direction, they will have a positive net worth in four months and be out of debt in 14 months. Once the Martins are out of debt, they will no longer have to pay $900.00 per month to service their debts. Of course, the Martins plan to put some of this money into saving for their children's college education.

The Martin's Future Net Worth Comparison Worksheet		
Monthly Change in Net Worth		$1,300.00
Multiply by 24 (months)	x	24
Result		$31,200.00
(Add) Net Worth from January	+	–$5,400.00
Future Net Worth in 2 Years		$25,800.00

The Martins' *starting place* was less favorable than Ann's, but their financial *direction* is positive.

The Martins' example is proof that the starting place of your financial journey is much less important than your direction. Their positive direction will make up for their less than desirable start over time.

Look at all of the possible outcomes of a financial journey. There are nine possible outcomes on page 71.

If charts aren't your bag, you can also think of these outcomes diagrammatically. The diagram to the right shows that your net worth represents your financial journey starting point. It also shows that the relationship between your income and expenses determines the direction of your journey.

Your starting point is the spiral in the middle representing your net worth calculation. The direction in which you are traveling is represented by the arrows pointing up or down. If your expenses are greater than your income, you will find yourself on the down arrow. Income greater than expenses? You are on the up arrow. If the difference between your income and expenses is zero, you are stuck in the center (for now).

What do you think of the possible outcomes? Hopefully these examples have illustrated the connection between your financial starting place (net worth) and your direction (income - expenses).

The Nine Financial Possibilities

Net Worth	Income - Expense =	Outcome
Negative	Negative	You are starting out in a less-than-favorable place and you are headed in the wrong direction
Zero	Negative	Your starting place is okay, but your direction is not good
Positive	Negative	You are starting out great, but you are losing ground
Negative	Zero	You are starting out in a less-than-favorable place and you have no direction
Zero	Zero	Decent start, but no direction
Positive	Zero	You are starting out great, but you aren't going anywhere
Negative	Positive	You are starting out in a less-than-favorable place, but you are headed out of it
Zero	Positive	Decent start, good direction
Positive	Positive	You are starting out great, and you are headed the right way

Establishing Your Direction — Money

**Exercise 4.1: Monthly Income and Expense Calculations
(45 minutes)**

To begin calculating your financial direction, we will use the Income Worksheet and the Expense Worksheet.

- ○ Enter monthly amounts into the Income Worksheet in all categories that apply to you. Personal Income should be your Net (after tax) Income.

- ○ In coming up with the specific amounts of your monthly expenses, consult your checkbook ledger. Look at the checks you have written and the automatic debits that have been made to your checking account. Use bank loan and credit card statements for the same purpose.

- ○ The items on the Expense Worksheet marked by an asterisk are those expenses which we normally think of on an annual basis. If you obtain an annual amount for any of these items, divide it by 12 before entering it onto the worksheet. For quarterly payments, divide the quarterly total by three.

- ○ Notice that the last item included on the Expense Worksheet is a "miscellaneous" category. This one can be wicked, because it is where we practice the greatest degree of self-deception, and it will be addressed in detail very shortly. For now, think of miscellaneous expenses as those everyday expenses for which you pay cash throughout the month.

- ○ Total both worksheets. Subtract the Expenses from Income in the box provided at the bottom of the Expense Worksheet.

Income Worksheet

Item	Amount	Item	Amount
Personal Income		Rental Income	
Alimony		Stock Dividends	
Child Support		Other	
		Total Income	

Expense Worksheet

Item	Amount	Item	Amount
Mortgage/Rent		Day Care/Babysitting	
Alimony		Club/Organization Dues	
Child Support		Medical/Health Insurance	
Automobile Payments		Prescriptions	
Credit Card Payments		Children's Tuition	
Equity Line Payments		Course Tuition (personal)	
Personal Loan Payments		Haircuts	
Student Loan Payments		Church Tithing	
Bank Fees		Vet Expenses	
Restaurants		Real Estate Taxes	
Entertainment		Gifts/Presents	
Hobbies/interests		Vacation	
Electric		Children's Clothing	
Gas - Home		Personal Clothing	
Water		Dental Visits	
Home Telephone		Doctor Visits	
Cell phone		Auto Insurance*	
Long Distance		Home Insurance*	
Internet Fees		Charitable Contributions *	
Gas - Auto		Home Repair/Maintenance*	
Cable TV		Subscriptions*	
Newspaper		Auto Licenses*	
Groceries		Tax Prep./Accountant*	
Children's Allowance		Legal Fees*	
House Cleaning		Safe Deposit Box Fees*	
Lawn Care		Miscellaneous	
Dry Cleaning		Expense Total	

Income (from pg. 72) - Expenses (From Above)

Exercise 4.1 CONTINUED

Just as in the fictional examples, you must apply the information from your monthly Income and Expense Worksheets to your Net Worth Worksheet #1(Chapter 3, Page 52) to create a second (adjusted) Net Worth Worksheet (Page 75) which will reflect:

○ Any increase in debt

○ Any decrease in debt

○ Any increase in savings

○ Any decrease in savings

To complete your second Net Worth Worksheet:

○ Subtract from items in the liability column the amount of the payments you made to them.

○ If your income is less than your expenses, you must reflect this difference by increasing one or more of the liabilities and/or decreasing one or more of the assets on your Net Worth Worksheet (just like Ann had to).

○ If your income is greater than your expenses, you must reflect this difference by adding to one or more of the assets and/or decreasing one or more of the liabilities on your Net Worth Worksheet (like the Martins).

○ Compare your first net worth result with your second net worth result. If your net worth has increased, you are heading in the right direction. If it has decreased, you are heading in the wrong direction. If it has stayed the same, you are stalled.

Exercise 4.1 CONTINUED

Net Worth Worksheet #2

Assets			Liabilities		
Item	Amount		Item	Amount	
Checking Accounts			Personal Loans		
Savings Accounts			Student Loans		
Stocks			Credit Cards		
Bonds			Other		
Certificates of Deposit			Other		
Mutual Funds			Other		
Retirement Accounts			Total		
Other					
Other					
Other					
Total					

Net Worth Calculation

Asset Total - Liability Total = Net Worth

Net Worth Comparison Worksheet

Net Worth Total #2

— Net Worth Total #1   -

Monthly Change in Net Worth

Well, what is the direction of your financial journey?

Special Notes

1. It is intuitively obvious that your monthly income must be greater than your expenses for you to be headed in the right direction, but this is only half of what you need to know. The actual number yielded by Net Worth Worksheet 1 subtracted from Net Worth Worksheet 2 is a vital piece of information because it not only shows you which direction you are traveling, but also the rate at which you're heading toward or away from your desired destination.

2. If your employer makes a contribution to your retirement plan via a payroll deduction, your retirement plan balance (an asset) will technically increase each month. It is better not to regard this as a liquid asset here, but it certainly is an important factor in reaching your final destination.

3. In Chapter 8, I will help you determine whether you are traveling at the optimum speed to allow you to reach your financial destination.

#$ Establishing Your Direction — Money

Exercise 4.2: Future Net Worth Calculation (10 minutes)

If you continue in your current direction, what will your net worth be in two years?

1. Take the difference between your total net worth in month one and your total net worth in month two from your Net Worth Comparison Worksheet.

2. Multiply that number by 24

3. Add the result to your net worth total from your Net Worth Worksheet #1 (Chapter 3, Page 52). This is your future net worth 2 years from now.

Future Net Worth Comparison Worksheet		
Monthly Change in Net Worth		
Multiply by 24 (months)	×	24
Result		
(Add) Net Worth from #1	+	
Future Net Worth in 2 Years		

You may be interested to know that the worksheets you have completed so far to measure your personal financial situation have all of the same components as those worksheets used by every business in America — large or small. They go by different names in the corporate world: the Net Worth Worksheet is called a Balance Sheet and the Monthly Income & Expense Worksheets form the corporation's Profit and Loss statement.

IBM, Coca-Cola, General Motors, Procter & Gamble and all the other corporations have to go through what you just did and they use the results to assess their companies' own financial journey.

Establishing Your Direction — Money

Exercise 4.3: Daily Expenditure Log (daily, for one month)

This log is really a device to help you verify the figures you provided on your Expense Worksheet. It is the only way that you can be assured that your Expense Worksheet numbers are valid. However, ***do not wait*** until you have finished your Daily Expenditure Log to complete your Expense Worksheet!

Be ready to be surprised at how much money you spend on the dreaded "miscellaneous" expense category. This log will be an essential tool in helping you reduce your monthly expenses.

Pick a day (it doesn't have to be the first day of the month), get out a piece of paper and start keeping track of ***every cent you spend on a daily basis.*** Everything. For a full month, list the amount of money spent and the item.

The Daily Expenditure Log does not have to be fancy. You can just write down the items purchased in a notebook or your program journal. I have included a sample for you to use if you wish.

What goes on the Daily Expenditure Log again? **Everything!** A can of soda? Yes. A pack of cigarettes? Yes. Movie ticket? Postage stamps? Lunch out? Candy bar? The $10.00 you give to your daughter at the mall? Yes, yes, yes, yes and yes. Everything goes on the list. After you have tallied the list at the end of the month, your Daily Expenditure Log will yield two very valuable pieces of information:

1. You will be able confirm (or amend) the entries made on the Expense Worksheet. Did you spend less on gasoline than you previously thought you did? Did you forget about the cable TV bill? Make the necessary adjustments on your worksheet.

2. You will now have information on how much you may have underestimated the "Miscellaneous" entry on your expense list. Miscellaneous expenditures are the items that, at first estimate, almost everyone cites as lower than they actually prove to be.

When you have compiled your Daily Expenditures Log, modify your Worksheet accordingly and take a break. You are done with worksheets and lists. 'Bout time, huh?

Daily Expenditure Log

Date	Payment Type	Item

Note: Payment Type = Cash, Checks, Credit Card, Debit Card, Etc.

Establishing Your Direction With Regard to Weight Loss

Time for some good news and some bad news. When it comes to establishing your direction with regard to weight loss, there are no charts to fill in. That is the good news. The answer lies inside you. You have to take a deep, honest look at yourself. That is the bad news.

Establishing Your Direction — Weight

Exercise 4.4: Which Direction are You Traveling In?
(A very painful five minutes)

Open your journal, take your pen in hand and answer these questions. If you continue functioning in terms of your "old" programs:

○ How much weight did you gain over the last two years? If that trend continues, how much weight will you gain in the next two years?

○ What health problems can you expect to encounter?

○ What will happen to your overall physical condition?

○ What will you see when you look in the mirror?

○ How will you feel about yourself?

How do you feel about your answers to the above questions? In the same way as it doesn't matter where you start your financial journey, it doesn't matter where you start with your weight journey — it is the **direction** that counts.

You might be satisfied with your weight now, but where are you heading? When it comes to weight, unlike with money, time is against you. As you age, your metabolism slows and sooner or later you are going to have to make conscious choices and changes.

If you are dissatisfied with your weight, that doesn't matter either. The moment you get on track you will feel better, for two reasons:

○ Better eating habits immediately support a positive mood change

○ Being constructive about your desired weight loss will raise your self-esteem

Establishing Your Direction — Weight

Exercise 4.5: Stating a Higher Intention (20 minutes)

It definitely isn't enough to want to lose weight. You are engaged in repro-gramming yourself and you need to amplify your thinking. You want to lose weight so that ... Fill in the blank.

You might have noticed in my weight story that when I stuck to the food intolerance diet and became my ideal weight, it was nothing to do with losing weight ... it was because I didn't want to pass my food intolerances on to my unborn child. The higher intention served as a program to sustain me.

> Recently a friend and colleague lost thirty pounds because he discovered that he was carrying the proverbial time bomb in his chest and he needed to reverse the condition of his arteries. He was not overweight by normal standards, but his cholesterol levels were too high. He did not want to die in his forties, leaving his wife and young children.
>
> He loaded himself up with all the new software he could find — in the form of all the diet and exercise information he could access — and followed a whole new program of diet and exercise. It is probably no coincidence, in terms of our computer analogy, that he had made his fortune designing software. Did I say "made his fortune?" Oh yes, this man retired in his early forties so that he could enjoy his family.
>
> When it was time to lose weight for health reasons, he went about it as sys-tematically as he had built his fortune. It was a pleasure to watch.

Write the answers to theses questions in your journal:

○ What is the "right" weight for you? How much weight do you need to lose?

○ Are you better off losing weight or getting fit?

○ Do you need to attend to either cholesterol, blood sugar or blood pressure issues?

○ What do you really want?

○ Do you suspect that you might have either food allergies or intolerances?

If you don't know about cholesterol, blood sugar, high blood pressure or food intolerances, do research on the Internet. For good information about blood sugar, you can consult Adele Puhn's book "The 5 Day Miracle Diet."

Establishing Your Direction — Weight

Exercise 4.6: Physical (one hour)

We urge you to speak to your physician. This is always necessary when beginning any weight or exercise program. If you are due, go for a complete physical.

Establishing Your Direction — Weight

Exercise 4.7: Consultation with a Fitness Professional (one hour)

We also recommend at least one session with someone specifically trained in the field of weight loss and **fitness**. This area has become a necessary science due to the national trend toward obesity and there is much to be learned from an individual consultation. The Surgeon General recommends one hour of moderately intense exercise on most days of the week.

Establishing Your Direction — Weight

Exercise 4.8: Keeping Track (10 minutes, daily)

Keep a log of what you eat. Yes, every morsel that crosses your lips. This is the one and only way you can keep track of what you're actually consuming.

Keeping a log is part of every successful diet program. If you don't want to carry two notebooks, keep your money log at the beginning and your food log at the end of the same notebook. (Sample — following page.)

The second burden is that you must keep track of portion sizes. You might be eating healthy food, but when it comes to weight, it is not only quality that counts, but also quantity.

All diets require that you "keep count." In the "counter" column track the item applicable to your chosen diet: calories, fat grams, carbohydrate grams, Weight Watchers® points, etc.

In the "quality" column put a (+) for high quality (organic) food, a (-) for junk food, including sugar & salt and a (0) for neutral foods — neither high quality nor junk.

Daily Food Log

Time	Food Item	Counter	Quality

Daily Exercise Log

Type of Exercise	Length of Time	Intensity of Workout

Exercise Intensity Guide

Light: No Sweat e.g. Walking, Stretching

Moderate: Light Sweat e.g. Fast Walking

High: Sweating e.g. Running

83

Action Notes

5 how to change

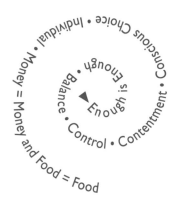

"If you really and truly don't want something, then it is the
preventive messages, the preventive activity in the brain, that
are necessary to insure that what you want to have stopped
is stopped. When those preventive messages are sent, there's
no way in which you're going to find yourself doing what you don't
want to do and don't intend to do. That is the crux of the matter."

Walter Carrington

If you are not succeeding, don't try again — that is, not until you have given
yourself a good reason to expect a different result.

In Chapter 2, you developed an understanding of how you are currently
programmed and in Chapters 3 and 4 you discovered the results that these programs have yielded. We have already noted that we can change our programs
by adding or deleting software and/or data.

The next step is to understand how you can change these programs. Your
greatest asset is the ability to exercise conscious choice. Sadly, if you don't harness your capacity for conscious choice, you are no better off than a robot or
animal. To harness conscious choice, you need to determine both what you do
want, and what you don't want, as well as identify your habitual patterns of
response. Then you must train yourself to **consciously** choose the new **wanted**
responses to the stimuli of life and prevent yourself from falling mindlessly into
the unwanted habitual responses.

Of course, the very act of reading this book and following our program of
how to lose weight and gain money is an act of reprogramming yourself. This
chapter will guide you through the steps required to bring about change.

Supporting Your Process of Change

Exercise 5.1: Identifying What You Need to Change (five minutes)

Put a check mark next to each of the following elements of the behavioral bridge that you need to address:

Weight   Money

_____   _____   Excessive Consumption

_____   _____   Imbalance between what's coming in and what's going out

_____   _____   Loss of Control

_____   _____   Comfort Seeking

_____   _____   Genetics and Family Patterns

_____   _____   Environmental Influences, including peer pressure, fashion and trends

_____   _____   Faulty equations in which Money = Love and Food = Love

As you read this chapter, look for techniques which can support your change process in each of the behaviors you have checked.

Why Help Is Necessary

Let's reconsider what we learned from Konrad Lorenz. He demonstrated that he could imprint baby ducks with the information that he was their mother. We humans are also imprinted by our experiences, both when they are repeated and when they happen at a critical period. As we have multiple experiences, we carry multiple imprints, which organize themselves, layer upon layer.

In addition to our multiple experiences, we are endowed with multiple faculties, as well as multiple aspects to our beings. In our culture, we recognize the physical, emotional, psychological, mental and spiritual aspects of our being.

Changing only one aspect of your being can put your system in conflict with the other aspects of your being. Humans are very complex, because we function both instinctively and consciously.

For example, if you want to lose weight, you can resolve mentally to stop eating sugar. However, if something upsets you emotionally and you need comfort, you might want to turn to ice cream. You can use your mental willpower to suppress your need for comfort, but don't be surprised if you wake up during the night, and groggily make for the freezer to eat a half-gallon of chocolate chip cookie dough.

By that same force of will, you may, for a few months, follow a new spending budget that is more aligned with your income, only to find yourself making multiple "comfort" purchases following an unusually stressful week at work.

Lasting change can only be effected by aligning all the aspects of your being along the same **intention**. Otherwise, the ignored aspects will play havoc with your plans.

Remember, you have become the way you are for good reason. You must take this into account or you will induce great inner conflict. The first step to change is accepting the current reality, the second step is giving yourself the respect you deserve for having made it so far and the third step is to formulate a rational and systematic plan of change, taking your **whole** self into account.

In systems theory, if you want to introduce change into the system, other aspects have to change also — it is highly unlikely that only one aspect will be found faulty and it can simply be removed and replaced — especially if you are trying to build an entirely new pattern of functioning.

Change is confronting and scary. What is familiar may be dysfunctional, but at least it is comfortable and known. We must not underestimate our fear of the unknown and our inability to handle sudden change.

For example, research on lottery winners has shown that they undergo immense stress. Their lives are not happier and many of them lose all the money that they won.

The Importance of Intention

Before you read more, I want to impress upon you the importance of intention. You may have already used some of the methods I am about to recommend, but not yet achieved the currently desired result. This does not mean the methods don't work. What it probably means is that you were not holding the intention that would systematically reorganize the data to yield this particular result. For example, if you have had psychotherapy to improve your relationship with your father, this will not have generalized into improving your ability to lose weight and gain money.

We can see the sense of this if we return to the computer analogy: to effectively use the computer, we need to load the appropriate software **and** we need to enter the data in a compatible fashion. To work effectively with numbers and create charts, we would want to use a number processing program not a word-processing program. We can create tables of numbers with a word processing program, but the process is laborious. It will be difficult to maintain the integrity of the data and impossible to manipulate the numbers, because word processing does not offer those options. However, the same data entered correctly into the number-processing program yields all kinds of possibilities with far less effort.

Your intention is what ensures that the data is entered correctly into the new program so that it can be effectively accessed and manipulated. Intention works because systems organize themselves around goals, using everything they know consciously and unconsciously. If we want to run up the stairs, we simply decide to run up the stairs and then our brain knows how to get the message through and put the whole system on "go" so that we find ourselves running up the stairs. We do not have to say to ourselves: "Breathe more deeply, lift the legs higher, go faster." We just say "Run!"

If you ask your brain to send a clear command, it will get the message through the system, **unless there is interference**. The clearer your intention is, the more effective your new programming will be.

Part of the process of supporting change is gaining that clarity of intention and part of the process is removing the interference.

Applying the Analogy

1. Eve wants to lose weight. She has had years of psychotherapy and has many insights into the origins of her weight problem. She has read hundreds of books on the subject and joined various weight loss groups, but she loses weight only to regain it. She has lost the same 15 pounds repeatedly.

   In this example Eve has identified and understood her programming, but has become stuck there because she has not identified the new program she desires. **"Losing weight" is not a program, it is the result of a program.** Nor has Eve intentionally loaded new software or intentionally entered new data. Both the new software and the new data are available to her — because she has read the books, had psychotherapy and attended support groups. We know that it isn't enough to purchase the software and have ready-to-enter data laid out next to the computer. To be effective, we must switch the computer on, actively load the program and then actively enter the new data.

   To move forward, Eve must choose an appropriate program for her to replace the old program. By talking to her therapist, she realizes that she has always wanted to study martial arts (loading new software), but because of her weight issues and poor body image, she has felt too self-conscious to join a class. Her therapist encourages her to at least investigate the possibility. When Eve arrives in class, she is comforted to discover that there are other women there who are even heavier than she (new data) and makes yet another discovery — due to her body type, she is above average in flexibility (re-entering of old data into a new program) — she is physically well suited to martial arts (new data).

   As Eve progresses through the martial arts program, she comes to feel completely differently about herself and her body. She begins to enjoy the capabilities of her body and begins to respect herself as an athlete — an entirely new body image. The bonus is that, because of the exercise, Eve's body firms and tones. She goes down two sizes and although she still weighs the same, this is muscle not fat! Eve has successfully re-entered old data and entered new data in a whole new program and has come out with much more than the original weight loss result she wanted.

If Eve had stayed with just wanting to lose weight, not only may she never have achieved the goal, but also she wouldn't have discovered her hidden talent for martial arts.

2. As you might have guessed, you can apply the concept of intention to your financial goals as well as your weight goals. The poor soul in Chapter 1, who went to the store to shop for a washer but ended up with a digital camera, probably thought that he had reorganized his software and data inputs with regard to spending money. After all, didn't he decide to put off buying the washer because he knew that his outstanding debt was already too high? Well, good for him. He saved the cost of the washer. Then what happened? He ended up with a purchase that he "wanted" versus one that he "needed." (And probably will have to go buy the washer next week as well.)

Instead of applying the firm, carefully thought out financial intention of "I'm not buying discretionary items until the necessities are taken care of," he allowed himself to revert to his unconscious, default intention of "I'll buy what makes me feel good." Well, at least he can take a picture of the old washer.

"It's our common experience of life that we go and do things and then we say, 'Oh, I didn't mean to do that, I didn't mean to do it like that, I didn't mean to do that at all.' We get into such a muddle, and at the core of the muddle is that we haven't made up our blessed minds. We haven't really been clear in our minds what we want and what we don't want. So if you half want something and half want something else, there's endless confusion."

Walter Carrington

Review of a Systematic Plan for Change

○ Identifying your current programming

○ Understanding how that programming occurred

○ Identifying what programming you desire

○ Loading new software

○ Re-entering the data/entering new data in a manner that is compatible with the desired programming

---

 Supporting Your Process of Change

Exercise 5.2: Making Up Your Mind (20 minutes)

Journal your thoughts about what kind of help you would like. Give yourself time to allow your deeper desires to come to the surface. Also journal your thoughts about what kind of help you **need**. What we "need" can be different from what we would like. We would probably like compassionate help, but what we need is a swift kick in the pants.

Resistance

The most important reason for getting assistance with any challenge is that we all suffer from resistance. Resistance is the reluctance or refusal to take action, even, and sometimes especially, when the action we are resisting is the very action that will make a difference. We dig in our heels or procrastinate rather than just get on with it.

If you are someone who can more easily take action to help someone else than to help yourself, there is no need to feel guilty. For some reason, cutting off our noses to spite our faces is a natural part of our human psychology. Only those who have achieved mastery seem to be able to do for themselves what they are already able to do for others, and even those who have achieved mastery in their specialty may find it challenging to work alone in a new area or discipline.

Recognizing your resistance and gaining insight into the causes is not sufficient. You must work at overcoming your resistance. Here are three possible methods:

- Schedule the action you are resisting for the time of day when your energy is highest

- Make an appointment with someone else who will help you face your resistance (for example, working out under the beady eye of a personal trainer)

- Make yourself accountable to someone else (by promising that you will have the action complete and ready for the other person by an agreed-upon date)

Resistance is what puts us in a cyclical battle of "should ... won't" with ourselves that causes us to get frustrated. Once we are frustrated, we become angry with ourselves, causing us to resist even more stubbornly. To break the cycle, we usually need the help of another person or support group. This help breaks up the resistance conversation and moves us forward into the ability to actualize our plans.

Supporting Your Process of Change

Exercise 5.3: Working with Resistance
(daily reflection for one week)

There are always hidden "benefits" to staying the way you are. These secondary benefits might not be as advantageous and appealing as the benefits of being your ideal weight or in a better financial situation, but if there were absolutely no benefits at all, you would have lost the weight and gained the money by now.

You might only think of one or two benefits at first, but the list will be long once you start recognizing the underlying secondary benefits. This is a very, very important list.

Here are two examples:

If I'm not my ideal weight/on track, I may as well eat ice cream, because right now it doesn't make any difference whether I do or don't. Benefit: I get to eat ice cream.

I was working at staying on a spending budget more fitting my income. One month, an unexpected expense came up. My budget is wrecked. Benefit: Now I will go out and buy whatever I want.

In your journal, generate a list, by doing a daily fast write on these questions:

❍ How do you benefit from avoiding your weight issues?

❍ How do you benefit from ignoring your poor financial situation?

Once you have started your list (remembering to add as you perceive more and more benefits — they will be legion) you will understand your resistance. At that point you will have become honest with yourself, and then you have hope of actually beginning that diet or new budget plan on Monday.

If you can't compile a list of benefits on your own, get help. Your best friend, spouse, a psychologist or counselor would be able to help you.

The Process of Change

To change we have to change. This sounds obvious stated in this way, but it is surprising how we all want the benefits of change to occur without us changing anything. Instead we keep trying and trying again, hoping for a new result. When I was a teenager, I was struck by the title of a song by Ellen McIlwaine: *Everybody wants to go to heaven, but nobody wants to die.*

If we want the "heaven" of losing weight and gaining money, we need to change, and "let die" the patterns of functioning which are producing the undesirable results.

We have already ascertained that these patterns have been established by our software programs and the way they have organized the data of our lives. Now we want to discover how we can change the programs and modify the data. There are many methods available to us. Some will be appropriate to you, others won't. You can choose what is appealing to you, but please note that the more methods you use, the more software you will be loading, the more ways of reorganizing and modifying your data will become available to you.

If you think that accessing these methods will be expensive, think about how expensive it will be for you if you do not change — and then decide whether you can or can't afford to move forward! It is important to be systematic and allow yourself to use different methods at different times in your life.

"If a man empties his purse into his head,
no man can take that away from him.
An investment in knowledge
always pays the best interest."

Benjamin Franklin

Psychotherapy and Counseling

Most of us are familiar with psychotherapy and counseling, but we usually only think of availing ourselves of these services when we are emotionally desperate.

We want to assure you that Psychology extends far beyond the field of moving people from dysfunctional behavior to functional behavior. The field of Psychology encompasses all areas of behavior and is singularly equipped to help you understand the origins of your patterns of functioning and how to change them.

Psychotherapy and counseling will help you understand the past and help you reframe the data of your life. If you would like to talk about why you are the way you are with an understanding listener who will not judge you, this might be the way for you to go.

Coaching

Many of us already understand why we are the way we are and we've gone over our past enough times. What we want is forward action with the guidance of someone who will listen to us, but keep us moving. We have also realized that the people who succeed in their careers are those who have had the luck to have high caliber teachers or mentors.

Coaching is a method for accessing the benefits of a teacher and mentor. Many coaches offer group workshops or seminars as a springboard, which are followed by individual sessions. There are also coaches who work with individuals. If you like the idea of a personal coach who will support you in actualizing your plans, you can access the names of organizations and personal coaches in the resource section of this book or go to our modern day source of information — the Internet.

The Alexander Technique

The Alexander Technique is a method for changing our patterns of functioning and is particularly useful for identifying and removing interference. This technique is usually associated with improving performance either in daily life to overcome patterns that cause pain, such as headaches or backaches, or to assist musicians, singers, actors and athletes in reaching their potential. While these represent the most common applications, the technique is much more far-reaching and significant than that.

Alexander, the founder of the technique, had a unique insight that if we want a different result, **we need to consciously stop doing the habit or pattern that is producing this undesirable result** to allow something different to happen.

Alexander lessons are taught on an individual basis and the teacher gives you an immediate experience of change as well as the conscious method for changing your habitual patterns.

You will probably be interested to know that the contents and understanding of this book come out of our knowledge and experience of the technique.

If you are a thinking person, you will enjoy finding out how a change in thinking manifests all manner of change in your life. And if you are a kinesthetic person (someone who learns through movement and action) you will enjoy discovering how different patterns of movement retrain your thinking and way of being.

Bodywork

Bodywork encompasses a whole category of techniques including Massage, Structural Integration/Rolfing®, Feldenkrais®, Trager work, Cranio-Sacral, Chiropractic, Reflexology, Body-Mind Centering® and a host of other methods which realign either the soft tissue or the skeleton. The premise is that we store our experiences and emotional reactions not only in our brains, but in all the cells of our bodies. By realigning and releasing the data that has affected our physical bodies, we can affect our psychology and bring about desirable physical, mental, emotional and spiritual changes.

The above list is incomplete and if you want this kind of work, find the most experienced, empathic practitioner available, who practices a method that appeals to you.

If you are someone who experiences emotion as pain in your body, or has difficulty verbally processing information, you might want to choose bodywork. Again, please refer to our resource appendix or use the Internet.

Courses and Training

Courses and training are a wonderful way to load software. Every time you learn, you are not only giving yourself a whole new way to categorize and access the existing data of your life, but also a whole new set of data.

Of course it is impossible to list all the courses and training opportunities that are available. What we want to emphasize is that you should support yourself in following your dreams. Ever wanted to learn to draw? Or sing? Do you feel short-changed because you never went to college? Take some time to see what is possible for you. And follow through. **You** know what you want to do — or always wished you had done.

Personal Growth Seminars

There are many organizations which offer personal growth training. If you enjoy intensive group experiences that have the potential of altering your life, you might want to consider such a program. Be sure to get a personal referral from someone you trust who knows you well. Beware of cultish organizations that draw you in with impossible promises. Remember that you are seeking to become more of an individual, actualizing your personal potential, not a sheep repeating mindless formulas.

Many of us benefit from these group experiences, using them as a foundation to go on to find teachers or mentors more personally tailored to our needs. I have already mentioned the possibility of coaching and that is both an alternative and additional route to consider.

Physical Training

We are increasingly recognizing that our culture has artificially separated our unified self into body and mind. Consequently, what was previously regarded as physical training turns out to be mental, psychological and emotional training as well. A good example of this is martial arts.

Methods aimed at stimulating brain development in brain damaged people have shown that neural pathways are established by taking these adults and children through physical patterns of movement. The truth is that all of us can stimulate our brains to higher functioning by learning patterns that seem to be physical in nature but develop new pathways and generally expanded functioning.

If you enjoy being physical, you may want to explore Martial Arts, Tai Chi, Yoga, Pilates, Dance or one of the many forms of movement training available. Whatever you choose, you can be certain that you will load new software and add new data.

Support Groups

If you want to lose weight or break addictive habit patterns you might want to join an organization, which specifically addresses the particular issue you battle. There are a multitude of twelve-step programs, which can help you with addictive tendencies ranging from alcohol and smoking to co-dependence and love addiction.

If you know you are struggling with programming that has been passed onto you by your family, do not let others deter you in your resolve to delete or modify the program.

I was heavily mocked for joining Weight Watchers® because I was not fat. Even the counselor at Weight Watchers® turned me away because I "didn't have five pounds to lose." I explained to her that although I was not currently overweight I could feel the pendulum swinging and without support I would gain another ten to twelve pounds.

I sat at Weight Watchers® looking at the many thin women who were there and thought to myself: "That woman isn't fat, what's she doing here? She must have a fat mother and be worried that that is going to happen to her." One day I realized that I was thinking about myself — I was one of those thin women with an overweight mother and that, because of the conversation in my family of origin, I feared putting on weight. I really enjoy going to Weight Watchers® meetings, because I am with a group of people who have decided to do something to change.

We didn't become the way we are on our own and it is highly unlikely that we can change the way we are on our own.

Who will you allow to help you change?

Supporting Your Process of Change

Exercise 5.4: Sifting Through the Choices (10 minutes)

Do some research to see what is available in your area and what appeals to you. The resource list in Appendix B will give you more ideas. Remember, it is unlikely that one approach will be enough. Here is a review of questions to ask yourself, to help you sift through the choices. (Psychotherapy, Coaching, the Alexander Technique, Body Work, Courses, Seminars, Physical Training, Support Groups)

Write a yes or no next to each question, then go back and rank the yes answers from 1-8, with 1 being the highest priority and 8 the lowest.

Y/N	Rank	
_____	_____	Do you need an understanding ear?
_____	_____	Do you need a teacher or a mentor?
_____	_____	Do you need direct help with changing your habitual patterns?
_____	_____	Do you store emotion and pain in your body?
_____	_____	Do you want to learn new skills?
_____	_____	Do you enjoy and benefit from group experiences?
_____	_____	Do you enjoy/need new physical forms of self-expression?
_____	_____	Do you need to address addictive patterns?

Exercise 5.4 CONTINUED

○ Look at your answers and see how they match up with the options, to support your process of change, described in this chapter and listed at the beginning of this exercise.

○ Look at the resource list in Appendix B.

○ Research the options that are available to you in your area. You can go to the local health food and book stores and see what flyers are on their boards. Look in your local alternative newspapers, which is generally where these kinds of practitioners advertise.

○ Speak to people you trust about who they can personally recommend.

Write your thought process and the results of your research in your journal.

Supporting Your Process of Change

Exercise 5.5: Entering New Data (three minutes!)

Choose the kind of help you want and make an appointment with the appropriate professional or commit to the class, course or program. Do not delay.

Keep a record: As you progress, journal your thought processes and decisions and maintain records of your insights and changes in thinking.

Action Notes

changing the direction
of your journey

"First, have a definite, clear, practical ideal
— a goal, an objective.
Second, have the necessary means
to achieve your ends
— wisdom, money, materials, and method.
Third, adjust all your means to that end."

Aristotle

We have discovered our programs, we have established our current direction
— and now we actually have to change! This is where we have to apply what
we've learned to address the following aspects of the bridge between weight loss
and money gain:

@ Loss of Control

@ Comfort Seeking

@ Excessive Consumption

@ Imbalance between what's coming in and what's going out

These changes cannot be accomplished without first taking back control
and instituting self-discipline. Hopefully, you have started using some of the
techniques in Chapter 5 to assist you.

Understanding Your Finances

Your Net Worth cannot change from month to month (let alone, year to year) without a change in your Income and Expenses during the same time period. **You cannot do anything** about your starting position. You are where you are. **You can change** your direction or, if you are already headed in the right direction, speed up your trip.

You can find all the information for changing direction in your Income and Expense Worksheets. If your income is smaller than your expenses, your direction will always be negative unless you change the balance.

You can change your direction from negative to positive in any one of four ways:

1. Increase Your Current Income

2. Utilize Your Current Income More Effectively

3. Decrease Your Current Expenses

4. All of the above

Increasing Income

The first option seems too obvious to be considered. "If I could receive more income, wouldn't I have already done so?" Well, maybe and maybe not. More income doesn't only mean being paid more for your current job. Perhaps you work in an environment where over-time compensation is available to you. Increasing your income might mean that you should consider taking a part-time job to augment your current income. Maybe your spouse should take a job for a period of time to get your family's financial journey headed in the right direction. Maybe your son should get a job to take some of the burden off your income. Maybe starting a business on the side is an option.

These are all possibilities. We expect that in doing this program your income is going to increase, because you will be instituting changes that will affect your whole being, including your earning capacity.

However, we believe that, in terms of the behavioral bridge between weight gain and money loss, **it is essential for you to first learn how to use your current income more efficiently.** Remember, we said earlier that statistics show that people who win the lottery are susceptible to losing their winnings. That can only be due to the "winners" not changing their pre-existing financial techniques to manage their new-found money.

Using Your Current Income More Effectively

You work very hard to earn your money. Doesn't it make sense to work equally as diligently to keep what you have earned?

This section is all about beating the system. What is the system? The system is that you don't feel that you have enough money to get by. You can beat the system by constantly reviewing ways in which you spend your current income.

Think back for a moment. Wasn't there a time in your life when you only dreamed of earning the amount of money you now earn?

Now you earn it, so why isn't it enough? It isn't enough because your expenses rose to meet (or exceed) each increase in your income. You need to pay attention to reprogramming yourself to utilize your current income more effectively or, **no matter how much you earn, you will never have enough.**

Let's look at a few ways of making your income stretch a little further:

Credit Cards

Do you use a credit card? Most people do, and statistics indicate that 61% of people carry a balance on their credit cards. One of the most emancipating parts of my personal financial journey was the day I paid off my credit card debt and knew that I would never carry a balance again. I was beating the system.

A credit card can facilitate certain types of transactions such as mail order, Internet purchases, etc. However, you only need ONE card. Get a credit card from a company that offers you something back at the end of each month besides a statement of what you owe them. The Discover® card offers a cash back plan to its cardholders. A percentage of every purchase you make with the card is given back to you periodically. Nice. Other credit cards allow you to earn frequent flyer miles on specific airlines for each of your purchases. If you travel by plane, this may interest you.

I suggest you do the following to all the rest of your credit cards:

1. Gather them together in a pile

2. Burn them

3. Take the ashes and bury them

4. Never visit the place where they are buried

Oh, by the way, this is not enough. They can and will rise from the ashes. The credit card companies will find you and resurrect your cards. The last step you must take is to call the credit card companies and cancel the cards. Only then will they truly be dead.

You are no doubt bombarded with solicitations from credit card companies enticing you to take on their cards and even more debt. Spend no time looking at these envelopes as they fall from your hand (unopened) into the wastebasket.

○ Make sure that you never carry a month-to-month balance on your one and only credit card.

○ Do not purchase anything on this card that you cannot pay for, in full, on the due date.

Harsh? A bit, but you will be much better off in the long run.

Debt Consolidation

If you are carrying debt in a variety of different forms (e.g. multiple credit cards, personal loans, store charge cards, etc.), consider taking out an equity line on your home to pay off all the other debts. You will still have the equity line to pay off. However, the interest rate on an equity line is normally very much lower than any rate you will find on the other forms of debt. And it carries an added bonus. The interest that you do have to pay on this loan is generally tax-deductible — another expense-saving benefit come April 15th of next year.

Savings

If you have managed to accumulate a balance in your savings account, this is good. However, if you put it into your savings account from your paycheck, it has already been taxed. It might make more sense for you to have your employer take the money out on a pre-tax basis and add it to your 401(k) plan or pension account. Some companies even offer a funds-matching plan wherein they will contribute so many cents to your account for every dollar you contribute. Ask your benefits department about your options.

Similar to the 401(k) idea, ask your employer if they offer a medical savings account plan. This also allows you to set aside tax-free funds for paying your medical bills.

Taxes

Are you self-employed? Schedule a meeting with your accountant to determine whether you have the most conducive business structure for taxes.

Remember to meet with your accountant on a regular basis. We all have to pay taxes, but there is no sense in paying more than necessary. Tax regulations change frequently. A good CPA will take a personal interest in your situation and make suggestions about how you can reduce your tax liability. But you also must remember to request this advice periodically.

Membership Benefits

For one annual fee, you can get multiple services and savings by taking up membership in appropriate organizations. Here are a few examples:

○ YMCA ○ AAA ○ Wholesale Clubs ○ Preferred Customer Programs

These are certainly not all of the ways to beat the system. Once you begin thinking this way, you will discover more money management insights by speaking to people, reading books and consulting experts.

Expense Reduction

Did you skip to this section because you feel you are optimizing your current income and you couldn't find any way to augment your income? If so, go back and review those two sections again. Face the discipline of thinking about these two possibilities. There are always ways to optimize and augment your income.

Here is the section where you have to exercise complete and absolute control over every item — expense reduction opportunities.

Look again at your Expense Worksheet. Every single item in that list is, **technically**, optional or discretionary. You don't **have** to have any of those items to live. Mortgage? No one forced you to buy a house. Auto loan? Ride the bus. Groceries? Work in a restaurant that will compensate you in free meals. Shall I continue? I didn't think so.

Do you think that these expense reduction suggestions are absurd? I sure do. I suggested them to put you in the frame of mind that every expense is negotiable. Certainly, I'm not suggesting that you sell your house (or leave your apartment) and set up a tent down by the river and live off the land. What I am suggesting is that you examine every expense with a jaundiced eye. Deal?

In a moment, I'm going to provide some examples of how you can reduce your monthly expenses without radically changing your lifestyle. Before I do that, I want you to be comfortable with the math I will use.

The Time Value of Money

I think I promised you at the beginning of this book that I would subject you to only one mathematical formula. It is the formula for computing compound interest *. I certainly didn't invent it. The Babylonians developed a form of it as early as 400 B.C.

I am going to demonstrate the math used to calculate how much each of your expense reductions will affect your net worth.

Here it is:

$$FV = A \left(\frac{(1+r)^n - 1}{r} \right)$$

Key

FV = Future Value of the Investment

A = Amount of Deposits

n = Number of Periods

r = Interest Rate

Yuck! Ugly, isn't it? Actually, when used to your advantage, it is one of the most beautiful things you've ever seen. In a bit, I'll let you know what Albert Einstein said about compound interest.

If mathematical formulas cause your mind to go blank, don't worry. I have provided "Quick Charts" for your use instead. The compound interest formula is for the convenience of those that want to play with the numbers.

Let's take an example that we can easily follow.

Suppose that I have $10.00 that I want to invest every month for five months at an annual interest rate of 6%, where the interest is computed — compounded — on a monthly basis.

6% is a fairly conservative interest rate. In my lifetime, rates have fluctuated between roughly 2% and 20%. I chose a rate applicable at the time of writing. I prefer to be realistic and conservative rather than fill your mind with extravagant expectations. To use another rate, just substitute it in the formula where we use 6%.

---

* My mother would be very upset with me if I lied to you. So, I am going to come clean. The official name of this formula is, technically, not the "Compound Interest Formula." Mathematicians generally refer to it as the formula for "The Accumulated Value of 1 per Period." Mathematicians are great at naming things! This formula does include the calculation of compound interest but is more complex because, not only is interest being compounded, but periodic contributions are also being made. So, for brevity's sake, I decided to refer to it here as the "Compound Interest Formula." Are you happy with that? Good. So is my mother.

○ The annual interest rate is 6%, but we will be computing the monthly interest, so we must divide the 6% by twelve.

○ 6% in decimal form is 0.06.

○ 0.06 divided by 12 is .005 — now we have our monthly interest factor. Let's do the math manually first.

Note that interest is generally computed and applied at the end of a given period. So, my first $10.00 does not gather any interest at all in the first month. However, at the end of the 2nd, my new balance is the total of the second $10.00 deposited, plus the 1st month's deposit (again, $10.00) **and** the amount of interest computed against the first month's $10.00 deposit ($.05, for a total of $20.05, with rounding). This pattern repeats itself until the end of the term (five months).

The chart below shows the extension of the math.

Compound Interest Demonstration			
Month	**Deposit**	**Interest**	**Balance**
1	$10.00	0.00	$10.00
2	$10.00	0.05	$20.05
3	$10.00	0.10	$30.15
4	$10.00	0.15	$40.30
5	$10.00	0.20	$50.50

Now, let's use the compound interest formula and see if we get the same result. Looking back at the formula, we need to assign value to all of the variables involved.

FV = The future value of my $10.00/month investment. That's what we're looking for.

A = The amount invested per month: $10.00

r = Interest rate = .005 which is the 6% interest (.06 in decimal form) divided by 12 to show the monthly rate

n = number of periods: 5 (Our investment time line is 5 months)

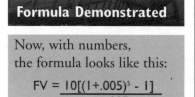

Formula Demonstrated

Now, with numbers,
the formula looks like this:

$$FV = \frac{10[(1+.005)^5 - 1]}{.005}$$

Use your calculator and do the math — or trust me.

FV = $50.50

Hey, they match!
I chose a very small time period for the above example so that the illustration of the manual computation would lend itself to fitting in a small space. If we had chosen our term to be 10 years instead of 5 months, we would have had a table extending 120 lines! The beauty of the compound interest formula is that it works for any number of time periods, large or small.

So, now, if you trust that the formula does in fact represent reality, we can go on to more realistic examples applying the formula.

Let's say that I find a way to invest $10.00 per month at an interest rate of 6%.

"The magic of compounding interest
is truly the eighth wonder of the world."

Albert Einstein

What happens after 10 years?

Put the numbers into the formula, like before.

FV = The future value of my $10.00/month investment. That's what we're looking for.

A = The amount invested per month: $10.00

r = Interest rate = .005 which is the 6% interest (.06 in decimal form) divided by 12 to show the monthly rate

n = number of periods: 120 (Our investment time line is 10 years — but the frequency in which we are investing is monthly, so the number of months is 10 times12 or120)

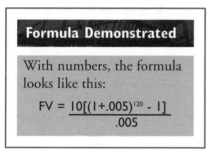

Formula Demonstrated

With numbers, the formula looks like this:

$$FV = \frac{10[(1+.005)^{120} - 1]}{.005}$$

Use your calculator and do the math — or trust me.

FV = $1,638.79

This shows that my $10.00 monthly investment (at 6%) is worth $1,638.79 after the 10 years. Is that a good deal?

Look at it another way. I contributed only $1,200.00 (120 months times the $10.00) to this $1,638.79 total. Our new friend "Compound Interest" provided the rest ($438.79). The $438.79 is 27% of the total. Compound interest works pretty hard for you.

It gets better. If you invest the same amount of money and allow the interest to compound for more years, the result is even more impressive.

Investing that same $10.00 at 6% interest for **twenty** years instead of ten would yield you $4,620.41. In this example you will have contributed just $2,400.00 toward your nest egg (20 years X 12 months/year X $10.00) while compound interest will have been responsible for $2,200.41 or 48% of the total yield. **The interest contributed almost as much to the total as you did.** That's the idea. The longer you let compound interest work to your advantage, the harder it works.

Okay, are you willing to look for ways to reduce your monthly expenses now that you know that for every $10.00 you shave off and invest, you will get back $4,620.41 in 20 years? I kinda thought so.

Every one of the entries in Quick Chart #1 on page 117 was calculated using the compound interest formula.

To use the chart, just pick the interest rate you want to use and the amount invested monthly, then read down the chart to see the result. This particular chart was specifically created to determine the value of a given investment at a given interest rate for a period of twenty years.

Let's see if Quick Chart #1 works as promised. Take the $10.00 monthly savings invested at 6%. Find the $10.00 invested on the left hand side of the chart. Find the interest rate (6%) along the top of the chart. Find the value in the chart where the two meet. The chart shows that the investment yields $4,620.41 — the same answer we just calculated by using the formula directly.

The Time Value of Money — Working Against You

Did some one just shout out that we're getting ahead of ourselves here? "How come we're talking about returns on investment when my net worth is negative?" "My expenses exceed my income. I don't have any extra money to invest."

You are correct. You probably won't be doing a substantial amount of investing until you get your net worth above zero. However, if your net worth is negative, it means that you almost surely owe someone money. If that someone is the local bank, guess what? They are using the same compound interest formula we just investigated. But, instead of paying you interest (as in the investment example), they are charging you that interest. (I spent 20 years working in a financial institution — this is how they make money).

Compound interest can work against you or for you. And, it gets worse. If the bank was willing to pay you a 6% interest rate on your money as an investment, you can be sure that they are charging you considerably more to borrow it.

Compound Interest

○ Working for you: Interest on your investments

○ Working against you: Bank charges

QUICK CHART #1
Value of given monthly dollar investment for a 20 year period at a selected interest rate

Amount Invested Monthly	Interest Rate					
	4%	6%	8%	10%	12%	14%
$5.00	$1,833.87	$2,310.20	$2,945.10	$3,796.84	$4,946.28	$6,505.83
$10.00	$3,667.75	$4,620.41	$5,890.20	$7,593.69	$9,892.55	$13,011.66
$15.00	$5,501.62	$6,930.61	$8,835.31	$11,390.53	$14,838.83	$19,517.49
$20.00	$7,335.49	$9,240.82	$11,780.41	$15,187.38	$19,785.11	$26,023.32
$25.00	$9,169.37	$11,551.02	$14,725.51	$18,984.22	$24,731.38	$32,529.15
$50.00	$18,338.73	$23,102.04	$29,451.02	$37,968.44	$49,462.77	$65,058.30
$75.00	$27,508.10	$34,653.07	$44,176.53	$56,952.66	$74,194.15	$97,587.45
$100.00	$36,677.46	$46,204.09	$58,902.04	$75,936.88	$98,925.54	$130,116.60

Expense Reduction Opportunities

Now you get to move on to the rewarding part — which of your own expenses can you reduce or eliminate? What will you collect after 20 years if you find a way to reduce your expenses and invest the money?

As mentioned, we will be using a 6% interest rate in the following calculations. However, as an illustration, I have included, in brackets, the value of the same savings/investment at 12% to give you an idea of the power of compound interest when rates increase.

○ Just how good does that $3.50 latte taste every day? How good does it taste after you find out that buying just two less per week would save you $12,900 [$25,800 at 12%] over the next twenty years? And what does that latte do to your waistline, by the way?

○ Going out for a night on the town once a week? Spending $50.00 each time? Cut that in two and the $100.00 you save every month will be worth about $46,000 [$92,000].

○ Do you want to increase your net worth and improve your health at the same time? Buy one less pack of cigarettes per week and the $16.00 (minimum) you save monthly will bring you $7,400 [$14,800].

○ Forego the last call drink, once every week. Pocket the $20.00 per month and have $9,200 [$18,200] to show for your discipline later.

○ Do you use coupons at the grocery store? If you did, and saved just $10.00 per month, the value of your clipping efforts would be worth almost $4,600 [$9,200] in 20 years. Get out your scissors!

○ How much does your cell-phone plan cost you? $35.00/month? Can you get by on the $20.00/month basic plan? If so, the $15.00 saved will net you over $6,900. [$13,800] (Of course, if you gave up the cell-phone altogether, you could "bank" $16,100 [$32,200] over the same time period. Can you remember the time in your life where you didn't have a cell phone — and actually survived? I can.)

○ Are you truly using all of the cable TV options that you were sold when you first subscribed? Cut them back to what you really use. Save $30.00/month and reap close to $13,800 [$27,600].

○ Are you in the market for a new car? Think about buying a nice used one instead or reducing the number of options on the new one. Shaving just $75.00 off your monthly car payment each time you buy a car will save you $34,600 [$69,200].

Got the idea? The expense reductions cited above add up to more than $135,000 [$270,000] over twenty years. Can you think of any reasons you might need that money in twenty years? If not, please kindly send it to me at... well, never mind.

Do you still think that the formula is ugly?

Changing The Direction Of Your Journey

Exercise 6.1: Personal Expense Reduction (one hour)

Okay, now it's your turn. You know your personal expenses better than I do.

○ Take a look back at your Expense Worksheet. Estimate the realistic amount of money you can remove from your expenditures

○ Put the amounts into the "magic" future value formula (or use the Quick Chart #1) and see what these expense reductions will mean to you down the road

○ This is a process. Give yourself time to deal with the prospect of spending less, but take action as soon as possible

By now, you should be convinced that relatively **small changes** in your daily spending patterns can yield **big results** down the road of your financial journey.

Changing The Direction Of Your Journey

Exercise 6.2: Preparing to Choose a New Diet
(20 minutes)

First you need to decide what setting supports you best. Take another look at the behaviors listed at the beginning of this chapter and check off the items that need your attention. Then consider which of the following can help you with your behavior:

○ Working with a friend

○ Working with a group of friends

○ Working with a personal trainer on a regular basis

○ Joining an organization, like Weight Watchers®, which offers a specific program

○ Joining a gym or health spa that offers exercise equipment as well as other services

Excessive consumption is a way of life in this country and you do want to examine your patterns of consumption. Not only do we tend to eat too much, we also eat whatever we want, whenever we want. Even if you don't overeat in terms of calories, that does not mean you aren't over-consuming pesticides, sugar, caffeine, alcohol, red meat and so on. Now is a good time to reprogram yourself to make better food choices by considering the following:

○ More whole foods, less refined foods

○ Less sugar

○ Less caffeine and alcohol

○ More organic foods

○ Less red meat

○ Less fat

○ Eating out less often

○ Planned grocery shopping

○ Taking care of your blood sugar levels

○ Less Salt

The next piece of the puzzle is to choose a new diet that will work for you. This will depend partially on what outcome you want and partially on your constitution.

As a researcher of diets for thirty years, I can assure you that every diet can help you lose weight, if you stick to it. The reason is that it is an eating program. As long as you are systematically following the program, you will lose weight. Diets stop working when you go off them and when you cheat. What you need to take into account is not whether the diet works, but whether the diet will work for you. The diet you choose needs to suit:

○ Your lifestyle   ○ Your temperament

○ Your preferences   ○ Your intention

○ Your body-type   ○ Your health risks

To get a good match, you can read a lot of books or surf the Internet. You need to choose a diet that fits in with your desired lifestyle and expresses your philosophy of life.

Remember, **you do have control** over what you put in your mouth, even if it doesn't feel that way sometimes.

Changing The Direction Of Your Journey

Exercise 6.3: Choosing a Diet (take one week, at least)

Oh yes! We've reached the part of the program where you need to choose a diet. Even if you don't think you have a weight problem and don't need to lose weight, you still need to look at how your diet reflects who you are — you are what you eat.

You have probably been investigating diet programs since reading Chapter 1 (or even longer!) Now it is time to choose. Here is the list again:

❍ Low fat ❍ Dean Ornish ❍ Eat Right for Your Type ❍ Vegetarian

❍ Macrobiotic ❍ Ayurvedic ❍ Organic/Whole Foods ❍ Weight Watchers®

❍ Atkins™/South Beach ❍ 5 Day Miracle Diet (Adele Puhn)

Special note: These are not recommendations. You must be responsible and make sure your diet takes care of your unique nutritional and health needs. Please consult a physician before changing to the diet you choose.

Every diet requires you to give up certain eating habits. The diet program you choose should allow you to continue eating the foods you can't possibly give up long term. Otherwise you are setting yourself up for failure. As you research the programs:

❍ Make lists in your journal of the restrictions each diet prescribes.

❍ Do not even think of combining aspects from the different diet programs. Each has its own principles for addressing health and wellbeing.

❍ Do not choose a faddish diet designed for quick weight loss.

❍ Match the diet program to the way you want to reprogram your eating patterns.

❍ Make a decent commitment, but if you discover you are better suited to a different program from the one you chose, you can change.

Write in your journal: Which diet did you choose and why?

Changing The Direction Of Your Journey

**Exercise 6.4: Integrate Your New Diet into Your Life
(180 minutes — over a week)**

Write down your plan, in detail.

> For example: When I get "scientific" about losing weight , I go to Weight Watchers®, I go to Pilates, I work out at the YMCA and I plan my meals and grocery shopping. I also have to be very careful to allocate time to food preparation or my whole plan tumbles.

Explain to yourself how you are going to:

1. Regain control

2. Institute self-discipline

3. Maintain a balance between what is coming in and what is going out

4. Align your energy

5. Limit consumption

6. Control addictions

7. Address genetic and family patterns

8. Cope with environmental influences

9. Prevent bingeing

10. Avoid the need to self-medicate

11. Feel loved

12. Reward yourself without using food to do so

Start your new diet — as soon as you have consulted your physician. Make that appointment NOW!

"On the plains of desperation,
    bleach the bones of countless millions,
  who — at the dawn of success —lay down to rest,
    and resting...died."

ACT

Action Notes

7

how to change
part 2 energy

"There are more things
in heaven and earth,
Horatio, than are dreamt of
in your philosophy."

Shakespeare

Earlier in the program, we introduced you to the electro-magnetic energy field, or aura, and likened it to the software of a computer. We deliberately didn't say much more than that, because we assumed that the concept of the aura is new for you. See if the information presented here is helpful.

If you decide you like the information but you aren't ready to believe in the existence of auras, that's fine. Let yourself use what is useful. You are welcome to reinterpret the information using any model of your choice. Other explanations for why these techniques work are equally worthwhile.

More understanding of the aura is important to us, as it is the equivalent of the software of a computer. Someone has to be able to design, write and modify software. Likewise it is essential to be able to tap directly into the aura to modify and align the energetic programs. Fortunately, there are now many professions which can provide this service. There are also techniques which you can use to help yourself.

This chapter will refer you to professionals who can reprogram your aura and give you a few specific techniques that you can do yourself.

Empowering Your New Direction

Which elements of the bridge between weight loss and money gain still need your attention? Put a check mark next to the elements which could benefit from support:

@ Excessive Consumption

@ Imbalance

@ Loss of Control

@ Comfort-Seeking

@ Genetics and Family Patterns

@ Environmental Influences

@ Money = Love and Food = Love

As in Chapter 5, when you read through this chapter, look for techniques that could help you.

Anatomy of the Aura 101

Our auras are most easily accessed by working with the **chakras**, which act as doorways to our energy system. We have seven major chakras, which are numbered 1 through 7. Each has a corresponding color of the rainbow and keynote energy.

In addition to these seven major chakras, there are another four significant chakras, corresponding to the palms of the hands and the soles of the feet. We also have hundreds of other chakras, because every joint in our body has a corresponding chakra point.

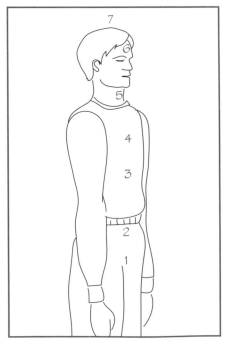

	Chakra	Color	Correlates to:
1	Root	Red	Survival, Anger, Creativity
2	Sacral	Orange	Emotions
3	Solar Plexus	Yellow	Will and Courage
4	Heart	Green	Love and Compassion
5	Throat	Sky Blue	Self-Expression
6	Third Eye	Indigo	Intuition
7	Crown	Violet	Intellect and Spirit

Anatomy of the Aura 101

Each of the seven major chakras gives rise to one of the seven layers of the aura. The root chakra corresponds to the physical body (considered the first layer of the aura) and the sacral chakra corresponds to the etheric layer of the aura. The next five layers are named according to the chakra name: solar plexus layer, heart layer, etc. In the integrated, healthy system, the chakras spin synchronously and the layers mingle harmoniously.

Energy healers are able to work directly on the aura, to clear energy, blend the layers and modify the spin of the chakras. These are the basic techniques and can be easily learned. More advanced methods of releasing trauma, reversing energy spirals, and identifying and healing blocks and "wounds," require in-depth training and practice.

For our purposes it is important to understand that since we have seven major chakras and seven layers to the aura, there are 49 points in the aura, which require attention. It is impossible for a single therapeutic or educational method to cover the development and alignment of all of these 49 points.

There is so much to us and so much to learn, that we do need multiple methods to find our way to full functioning.

Empowering Your New Direction

Exercise 7.1: Clearing Your Aura (two minutes)

Here are two methods you can use to clear your own aura:

1. Intentionally brush your whole body down with your hands, as though you are brushing lint off your clothes. Don't forget your head, back and backs of your legs. Shake the "lint" off your hands, imagining that the "dirt" is transforming into sparkles of white light. Repeat three times. This is especially helpful if you have been in crowds, working with a group of people or seeing people one after the other and have collected their projected energy.

2. In the shower, soap yourself and rinse off, holding the conscious intention to clear your aura. Be sure also to comb or brush your hair. (The conscious intention is the essential ingredient, in the same way as getting gum off your shoe requires more than the habitual wipe on the doormat.)

Clearing your aura will help you to feel calmer, lighter and more focused. We recommend that you use this method any time that you feel your self-control is slipping, or you feel a disruption in your energy.

The Money Spot

Money relates to the third chakra, the solar plexus. The color, yellow, and the name of the solar plexus relate this chakra to the sun, the original source of all our energy. The higher color of the solar plexus is gold. The solar plexus is the chakra of will and courage, and clearly, also of money. The "money spot" in the aura, that is, the spot that relates directly to the ability to acquire money, should be located above the physical solar plexus, in the 3rd layer of the aura, which is the layer of the solar plexus. The drawings will help to clarify this.

Empowering Your New Direction

Exercise 7.2: Assessing the Money Spot (five minutes)

Assessing the Money Spot		
Rating	**Placement**	**Qualities**
Healthy	Correctly placed in the aura	Open/Receptive Massage of this spot yields money in 1 - 3 days
Under-Active	Can shrink or be displaced in the aura	Realignment and repeated "massage" of the under-active money spot will be needed to yield acquisition of money
Over-Active	Bloated, eclipses other aspects of the solar plexus, as well as the second chakra (emotional) and heart (love and generosity)	Realignment and energizing of other chakras needed to bring other aspects of life and self-expression into balance

We don't expect you to be able to assess your money spot on your own, but you can take an educated guess (knowing your own tendencies).

Rate your money spot:

> Healthy   Under-Active   Bloated

The Weight Spot

The weight spot is located in the intellectual/spiritual (7th and outermost) layer of the aura, at a location where three points from the physical body converge:

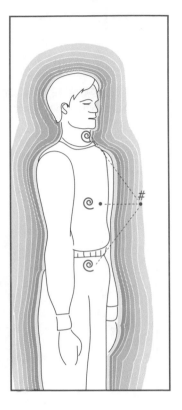

- ○ The throat chakra   (self-expression)

- ○ The sacral chakra   (emotion)

- ○ The pancreas   (sugar metabolism)

This indicates that our weight is influenced by the interaction of our functions of emotion, self-expression and the ability to metabolize sugar, all of which are being governed by our intellectual and spiritual process. No wonder it isn't simple to lose weight!

It is also interesting to note that the pancreas is considered the alternate location of the solar plexus chakra, once again confirming the strong energetic relationship between weight and money.

Empowering Your New Direction

Exercise 7.3: Assessing Your Weight Spot (five minutes)

Without training, it would be even more difficult for you to find and assess your weight spot than your money spot. But you can accurately assess the energetic quality of your weight spot by answering the following questions in your journal:

1. Do you take care to keep your blood sugar at the desirable level by eating regularly and on time?

2. Are you subject to yo-yo dieting?

3. Do you follow a regular exercise routine?

4. Are you too rigid and over-disciplined?

Assessing Your Weight Spot	
Properties of the Weight Spot	**Indicative of**
Firm and Stable	Routine and System
Spongy	Irregular and Sporadic Efforts
Loose and Wavy	Lack of System and Routine
Brittle	Rigid Discipline

What is the likely rating for your weight spot?

Firm   Spongy   Loose   Brittle

Finding An Energy Healer

Systems of energy healing and books on the subject currently proliferate. One of the better-known methods for working on the aura is called "Healing Touch" and many nurses and massage therapists are awarded CEU's (Continuing Education Units) for training in this technique. Other well-known teachers and authors of books on energy healing techniques include Barbara Brennan, Carolyn Myss and Rosalyn Bruyere. (Check Appendix B for resources.)

Energy healing techniques have certain features in common:

○ You are taken into an altered state of consciousness in which you relax deeply

○ An effective session leaves you feeling refreshed and revitalized

○ Each of the seven elements of the behavioral bridge can be addressed because these techniques work directly with the software programs that have been loaded into your aura

If you would like to experience the benefits of energy healing, a personal referral is definitely the best way to locate a practitioner. If you have to choose from a list, look for a professional practitioner who has good background qualifications (like a college degree) as well as adequate training in energy techniques. Here are two guidelines:

1. A weekend of training does not make a professional. A college degree, extensive post-graduate training and hands-on experience make a professional.

2. There are also gifted practitioners who have learned their skills the hardest way of all — by healing themselves. Healing can be especially powerful if you go to a practitioner who has traveled a similar journey to the one you need to travel.

When you call a practitioner to find out more about the service being offered, it is acceptable to ask how she trained and what brought her personally to this work.

More Techniques for Changing Energy

There are many techniques for changing energy, including all the methods of vibrational medicine (acupuncture, homeopathy, naturopathy, herbalism, flower essences, color therapy, Reiki, etc.) so we will just touch on a few that we know well. Once again, we do want to encourage you to choose the methods that appeal to you.

Crystals

Crystals are superb devices for reprogramming our energy. They also carry programs that can load us with new software.

If you are interested in crystals, there are two ways you can benefit from their properties:

○ You can purchase crystals to wear or put in your environment

○ You can go to a crystal healer

No knowledge is required for you to make an excellent crystal purchase, because the crystal will choose you! All you need to do is go to a store that sells crystals or go to one of the gem and mineral shows. Walk around and see what "calls" you. You may be surprised to find that the crystal you find irresistible, is not the one you most like the look of. Crystals are a lot like people — there are those you admire from afar and then there are those you want to be friends with.

Once you are wearing the crystal, or have placed it in your environment, it will affect you subtly by loading you with new software. Don't be surprised if your attitude shifts, your thinking suddenly changes or you develop a new understanding of a situation that has been challenging you.

Crystals for Money Gain

Topaz, citrine and adamite are three of the minerals associated with attracting money. Manifestation crystals — crystals which have another crystal inside them — and bridge crystals — crystals which have another crystal partially inside them — can be used to consciously manifest abundance.

Just having a crystal with these properties is not enough. You need to actively program the crystal through guided meditation with specific, responsible instructions. For example, you do not want to request to manifest $100,000, only to have a beloved relative die and leave you the money. Also, if you are working, you will manifest $100,000, but this might be your usual income over time, not the extra you were hoping for. Instead of saying: "I want to manifest $100,000," you can say: "I want to manifest an extra $100,000 in a way that brings no harm to anyone else, or myself, but by finding safe methods of increasing my income and having my investments yield more interest."

Once the crystal has loaded you with the program, you will discover that when the opportunities arise, you will now recognize them and make choices and decisions that lead to the manifestation of what you have requested.

Crystals for Weight Control

The following crystals can help you specifically with weight loss: Chrysocolla, Diaspor, Heulandite, Picasso stone and Green Tourmaline.

Crystals have many properties and support our energy on multiple levels. I have listed crystals that have the specific properties of attracting money and assisting weight loss, but a crystal that attunes your individual energy will strengthen and support you in all aspects of your life, including your ability to lose weight and gain money.

If you want to access crystal healing, you will need to find a crystal healer. Many people are trained in this technique and it should not be hard to find someone. Again, apply the same discriminating standards that are suggested for finding an Energy Healer.

A point that is worthy of note is that crystal is one of the elements that make your computer work.

Aromatherapy

Aromatherapy is the art of using essential oils for reprogramming energy. The oils can enter your system either through your nose, which is a direct doorway to the brain, or by application to the skin (preferably where there is fatty tissue that will dissolve the oil) whereby it travels into the bloodstream, directly affecting the chemistry of your body. Aromatherapy is a very powerful way to shift mood and attitude. It is another method for both loading software and changing data, especially allowing data release and data modification.

Oils for Money Gain and Weight Loss

Oils for attracting money include: Cinnamon, Galangal, Oakmoss, Orris, Tonka and Vetiver. None of the references on aromatherapy oils that I consulted make a specific recommendation for weight loss. To use aromatherapy oils to support weight loss, you need to ascertain the specific issues — such as self-esteem, self-love, addiction, stress — that contribute to the symptom of weight gain and then use the appropriate oil(s).

Most of the vendors who sell aromatherapy oils also sell ready-made blends for abundance and for appetite control.

Combining Crystals and Aromatherapy

I have had great success combining crystal properties and essential oil properties to make special blends assisting with abundance and appetite balance. One customer, who bought the abundance blend, called to say that within a week she received a check for $1000 from a relative who had never given her money before. The note accompanying the check explained that the money was to support her in the courageous actions she was currently undertaking.

Another customer called to say she had unexpectedly received a check for $20,000 on the seventh day of using the cream!

These are some of the experiences that have led me to understand how the aura carries a program which organizes our lives and that, once we understand how to load new programs and change old ones, we can bring about the changes we want.

DNA Reprogramming

This is a relatively new energetic method started by a woman, Vianna Stibel, who learned how to reprogram her DNA when she was diagnosed with cancer. We all know the part that DNA plays in influencing our physical and mental make-up. Vianna was able to heal herself of her illness by reprogramming her DNA.

I recently learned this technique myself and, as a trained psychologist, I was skeptical. I could see this might work for shifting beliefs, but I couldn't imagine how this could work for inherited disease. However, the techniques are quick and painless, so I agreed to try them on a friend of mine who has a genetic liver disorder and had been told he would need a liver transplant. When I saw him again six months later, he had just been told by his surgeon that he may never need a transplant because his liver was showing five out of the seven signs that indicate healing.

I would never recommend that one use a technique like this for a physical condition **instead** of medical care, but I do think taking advantage of every possible method available makes sense too.

This technique can help you systematically "pull" and clear the inherited beliefs that govern your relationship with weight and money and reprogram you, as the name suggests.

Feng Shui

Feng Shui is the Chinese art of placement and is a systematic method for organizing the components of your home (or office) to create an energy flow that will support health, mood and finances. Conversely, poor placement can disrupt the energy lines and create blockages and interference.

Feng Shui is a method of changing the exterior (the environment) to bring about changes on the interior (your self), that has been enjoying increasing popularity. You can readily access this information in books, but if you suspect that the structure of your home is lending itself to a negative program, I would recommend a qualified practitioner.

You certainly don't have to wait to tidy up, throw away clutter and fix what is broken. I find nothing quite as disturbing to my energy as piles of paper, mounds of clothes, burnt out light bulbs that haven't been replaced and the accumulated disorder of daily living. When my space is reasonably organized and aligned, I am able to think more clearly and function better. I can also find what I'm looking for.

We spoke to a Feng Shui consultant, trained in the *Compass and Flying Stars* school of Feng Shui, the authentic Chinese method. Our consultant recommended the following methods for realigning your relationship with weight loss and money gain.

Feng Shui for Money Gain

1. Using a compass, locate the southeast portion of your house. Place a moving water feature, which includes a bowl — like a fountain or a fish bowl with a fish in it — in this portion of your home. The movement of the water enhances money flow and the bowl enhances accumulation.

2. Looking at the entire lot on which your home is placed, locate the southeast portion. Plant or place purple flowers and/or a mound of amethyst (purple stones) in this area. You can also sprinkle Chinese money, I Ching coins, in this area. The purple flowers and stones and the coins attract wealth.

3. Feng Shui is a sophisticated art and you may want to bring in a qualified consultant who can tap the "money stars" in your home. You can expect immediate results if the technique has been effective. Our consultant has witnessed clients inheriting property, receiving checks in the mail and acquiring jobs within three days. The money stars need to be reactivated on a monthly basis.

Feng Shui for Weight-Loss

1. Clear clutter and unneeded possessions. The rule is: *use it, love it or toss it.* Everything beyond that is **additional weight on you.**

2. Use your kitchen only for preparing meals. Don't hang out in the kitchen and don't argue in the kitchen. Eat in your dining room. The reason for this is that every time you see your refrigerator, you are implanting the thought of food in your head. If you have the choice, don't leave or enter your house through the kitchen. Use another access, like the front door.

3. Locate the center of your home. This area needs to be clean and strong. Do not clutter this space. Use colors such as yellow, tan and red to decorate this area and materials such as ceramic and brick to denote the properties of strength.

Additional Influences Which Program You

We have already seen that everything we do in life affects us, but there are at least two other influences which can supply surprising information that can change the way you understand yourself, as well as help you change your programming.

Astrology

If you are having trouble unraveling your own behavior, you might want to get a reading of your astrological chart. To get your astrological chart done, you need your exact time and place of birth and a reputable astrologer. If you can't access your time of birth, a good astrologer can interview you for pertinent information, match your propensities to which planet would have brought this influence, and thereby establish your time of birth.

In choosing an astrologer, you definitely want to go with a personal recommendation. A less expensive, but informative way to go, is to access a computer program that yields an astrological reading. This will give you a great deal of information, but will not personalize and explain the data the way an astrologer can. Remember to let the astrologer know that you are particularly interested in applying the information to your weight and money issues.

Horoscopes have given astrology a bad rap. All kinds of mysteries about my life were cleared up in one session with an astrologer, when she explained how the alignment of the planets at the time of my birth had programmed me. The astrologer was careful to explain that while my chart represented a map of my life, it was not deterministic. Once I understood the influences, I was able to make choices that could help address the weaknesses of the program, as well as utilize the strengths.

For example, the overall diagram of my chart was a three-legged table. This missing leg represented the physical body, indicating that my physical body was the weakest aspect of my being. I found this out at the time that I was training to be an Alexander teacher. The information confirmed that I had made an excellent choice because the Alexander Technique would give me lifelong support in addressing this weakness. If I had stayed with my original career choice, Clinical Psychology, my career would not have been able to help me with the missing table leg.

Astrologers can also take your personal data and check the movements of the planets in a given time period, letting you know advantageous and disadvantageous times for instituting your plans.

Past Lives

We are not programmed only by the forces of this lifetime, but by the forces of all of our previous lives. It can be very confronting to think that we not only spend this life repeating the same patterns, but that we have been repeating these patterns for centuries!

There is a great amount of information available to us about our current lives, so we don't have to go rooting around for more justification about the way we are, as in "I died in a concentration camp during World War II and that is why I am obsessed with food and money."

On the other hand, if you have been systematic about reprogramming yourself and you're not getting the alignment you desire, you may be able to change your frustrating patterns through discovering the past life influences that are still programming you in this lifetime.

You can go either to a past-life regression therapist who will hypnotize you so you can access your past-life memories, or an intuitive practitioner who is able to "see" your past lives and tell you what you have experienced.

What Does All This Mean?

Does this mean that to lose weight and gain money you have to reprogram your DNA, get your aura cleaned, buy a crystal, rub oil on your body and redecorate your house? NO!

These are some methods that will assist you in reprogramming yourself. You should only choose what appeals to you and what is comfortable, but remember that the more techniques you use, the more successful you will be, in the same way as the more courses you take, the more you learn.

Does this mean that if you apply the insights from an astrological reading, buy and work with a manifestation crystal, use abundance cream and reorganize your furniture, you will lose weight and gain money, even if you don't believe in what you're doing? YES!

Even if you aren't a believer, these methods will work. The earth has always been round, even when people believed it was flat. Try it, you'll like it!

 Empowering Your New Direction

Exercise 7.4: Go to the Library or Bookstore (three hours)

Find several general texts on alternative medicine and read up on the techniques, which attract you.

Choose at least one method to assist you in changing your software.

Empowering Your New Direction

Exercise 7.5: Integrate Some of the Techniques into Your Life (30 minutes)

Here are some examples:

○ Unclutter one room or area (like a desk or drawer) of your home

○ Place a fountain in the southeast portion of your home

○ Buy a citrine crystal. Hold it in your hand and meditate on attracting money. Place the stone on your bedside table where it can affect your energy

○ Develop a routine of clearing your aura before going to bed

○ Acquire a crystal pendant that will support you in your weight loss program

○ Ascertain the issues that contribute to your weight gain and money loss, and acquire the aromatherapy oils that will shift your energy in the desired direction

○ Make an appointment with an appropriately qualified practitioner

Write down a plan in your journal and continue to journal your experiences and changes in thinking.

Action Notes

8

will you reach your destination?

"You can't manage what you can't measure."

Willaim Hewlett

Now you should focus your interest on finding out if your starting point, teamed with a good direction, will get you to the desired end of your journey. It might not. You could lose ground, slow down, or suddenly run out of gas.

We covered some ways to make the change in your direction from negative to positive. Next you need to work backwards from your goal to ensure that you have got all the means in place to achieve that goal.

Managing Your Finances

John Paul Getty recommended: "Rise early, work late, strike oil." Do you concur with Mr. Getty's suggestion for planning your financial future? Unfortunately, most of us must develop a plan that's a lot more detailed than capping some gusher in Texas.

Everybody's financial destination has one feature in common — a specific amount of money at a specific time in the future. One person might say, "I will need $150,000 in 15 years to send my daughter to college." Another might plan to retire in 25 years and needs an additional $300,000 in savings, over and above Social Security and his pension.

- ○ Do you have a retirement age in mind or an age at which you want to cut back on your work?

- ○ Do you have children whose education you would like to fund down the road?

These are examples of financial journey destinations. You could have another destination.

Whatever your personal destination requires, you probably have asked yourself: "How can I be sure that I will reach my destination?" Good question. Let's look at how to find out.

Calculating Your Retirement Sum

How much money must you invest on a monthly basis now to ensure that you have the resources to reach your destination in the future? There are mathematical formulas to help you calculate that number …

What? Oh, I promised to introduce you to only one formula in this book and I've already done that. Okay, we'll just use more "Quick Charts." The formulas which support the entries in the Quick Charts are kissing cousins to the Compound Interest formula anyway, so they're not that exciting to see.

Take a look at Quick Chart #2 on page 149. It can be used as a shortcut to determine how much money an individual must invest on a monthly basis (at a chosen interest rate) to yield a desired return. As we discovered in Chapter 6, the length of time that the investment interest is allowed to compound has a great effect on the end result. In this particular chart, the investment time frame used is 30 years (The reason for my choosing a 30 year period will be evident in a moment.) Shorter or longer time frames would yield smaller or larger returns for each given interest rate. There are additional quick charts for shorter time frames in Appendix A. If the charts you require do not appear in this book, consult our website www.loseweightgainmoney.com.

Along the top of the chart you can see various interest rates from 4% to 14%. Along the side you see the amount of money you desire to accumulate. Where the two meet in the chart is the amount of money you need to invest on a monthly basis to achieve the desired savings in 30 years' time.

For example, let's stick with our 6% interest rate. If you wish to accumulate $250,000 over the next 30 years, follow the 6% column down until you get to the row with $250,000 in it. The amount you must contribute monthly and invest at 6% to yield the $250,000 is $248.88.

Determine the amount you wish to save. Find that amount in the "savings sum" column. Select the interest rate that is available to you. Where the two meet in the chart indicates the amount you need to save monthly. Please note that the investment time period in this chart is 30 years.

QUICK CHART #2
Monthly Investment Needed To Return A Savings Sum In 30 Years At a Given Interest Rate

Savings Sum	Interest Rate					
	4%	6%	8%	10%	12%	14%
$50,000.00	$72.04	$49.78	$33.55	$22.12	$14.31	$9.10
$100,000.00	$144.08	$99.55	$67.10	$44.24	$28.61	$18.21
$150,000.00	$216.12	$149.33	$100.65	$66.36	$42.92	$27.31
$200,000.00	$288.16	$199.10	$134.20	$88.48	$57.23	$36.41
$250,000.00	$360.20	$248.88	$167.74	$110.60	$71.53	$45.51
$300,000.00	$432.25	$298.65	$201.29	$132.71	$85.84	$54.62
$350,000.00	$504.29	$348.43	$234.84	$154.83	$100.14	$63.72
$400,000.00	$576.33	$398.20	$268.39	$176.95	$114.45	$72.82
$500,000.00	$720.41	$497.75	$335.49	$221.19	$143.06	$91.03
$525,000.00	$756.43	$522.64	$352.26	$232.25	$150.22	$95.58
$750,000.00	$1,080.61	$746.63	$503.23	$331.79	$214.59	$136.54
$1,000,000.00	$1,440.82	$995.51	$670.98	$442.38	$286.13	$182.05

Now that you've seen how this chart works, let's look at an applied example:

Jacqueline has been doing some homework on her retirement. She is currently 35 years old. She hopes to retire at age 65. She wants to be able to depend on her retirement money lasting until she is 90 years old.

Jackie (that's how she prefers to be addressed) currently earns $3,600.00 per month and that is enough for her to live on comfortably. But how much money must she accumulate before retirement time to allow herself to maintain her lifestyle after retirement?

First, Jackie needs to calculate what she will need to live on when she retires — 30 years down the road.

We will assume that Jackie availed herself of professional help who calculated that she will need approximately $6,500 per month to cover her living expenses in order to maintain a satisfactory lifestyle until she is 90 years old (25 years after retiring). She has 30 years to get herself prepared. That is plenty of time.

Let's assemble the pieces:

○ Jackie wishes to retire in 30 years

○ She wants her retirement nest egg to last 25 years

○ She has been notified by the Social Security Administration that her benefit from that source upon her retirement will be $1,500.00 per month *

○ Her employer has advised her that the estimated value of her 401(k) plan at retirement will be $250,000.00

How much does Jacqueline need to save on a monthly basis to meet her retirement objectives?

---

* The Social Security Administration, in 1999, began notifying workers of the amount that they could expect to receive in monthly benefits at retirement if their earnings continued at their current pace. If you pay Social Security Taxes, you probably receive these notifications on a quarterly basis. If not, you can contact the Administration at 1-800-772-1213 or www.ssn.gov to arrange to be informed of your future benefits.

First we need to get everything reduced to the same basis.

For Jackie to have $6,500.00 per month to spend for 25 years, she needs to have $1,950,000.00 (25 years X 12 months X $6,500) at retirement. Does this seem like a lot of money? Well, it seems like a lot of money because it is … **and it is wrong!**

We didn't take into account the compound interest effect. When Jackie retires, will she spend her entire available savings in the first month? Not likely. She will use the $6,500 she needs and the rest will continue accumulating interest.

So let's start again:

○ Jackie wishes to retire in 30 years

○ She wants her retirement nest egg to last 25 years

○ Jackie needs $6,500.00 per month for retirement comfort

○ Social Security will cover $1,500.00 of that amount

○ Her 401 K plan will provide her $250,000.00 in a lump sum at retirement

Jackie needs to make up the difference between her needs ($6,500) and Social Security's contribution ($1,500). That leaves $5,000 per month required between her 401(k) and her savings.

Now, at retirement, Jackie will be taking money out of her 401(k) to live on. However, interest on the remaining funds in the account will still garner interest. The formula used to see how much money can be taken out every month while still applying interest (6%) to the remaining and have the original principal ($250,000) last the required number of years (25) is a version of a formula called "The Present Value of 1 Per Period." Those math dudes are an exciting group aren't they? Does the name give you a nasty feeling? Not to worry. I used the formula. You get to use more Quick Charts.

Take a look at Quick Chart #3 on the next page.

QUICK CHART #3
Monthly Return Of Lump Sum Over 25 Years At Selected Interest Rate

Lump Sum	Interest Rate					
	4%	6%	8%	10%	12%	14%
$100,000.00	$527.84	$644.30	$771.82	$908.70	$1,053.22	$1,203.76
$150,000.00	$791.76	$966.45	$1,157.72	$1,363.05	$1,579.84	$1,805.64
$200,000.00	$1,055.67	$1,288.60	$1,543.63	$1,817.40	$2,106.45	$2,407.52
$250,000.00	$1,319.59	$1,610.75	$1,929.54	$2,271.75	$2,633.06	$3,009.40
$300,000.00	$1,583.51	$1,932.90	$2,315.45	$2,726.10	$3,159.67	$3,611.28
$350,000.00	$1,847.43	$2,255.05	$2,701.36	$3,180.45	$3,686.28	$4,213.16
$400,000.00	$2,111.35	$2,577.21	$3,087.26	$3,634.80	$4,212.90	$4,815.04
$450,000.00	$2,375.27	$2,899.36	$3,473.17	$4,089.15	$4,739.51	$5,416.92
$500,000.00	$2,639.18	$3,221.51	$3,859.08	$4,543.50	$5,266.12	$6,018.81
$1,000,000.00	$6,059.80	$7,164.31	$8,364.40	$9,650.22	$11,010.86	$12,435.21

○ How much does Jackie have in her 401(k) account at retirement? $250,000, right?

○ Find that amount in the leftmost column.

○ What is our assumed rate of interest? 6%, right? Find that column across the top of the chart.

○ Find where they meet. The figure is $1,610.75.

○ Jackie's $250,000 will provide $1,610.75 per month for the desired 25 years.

Now where is she?

○ Money needed per month: $6,500.00

○ Social Security's contribution per month: $1,500.00

○ 401(k) account monthly contri-bution: $1,610.75

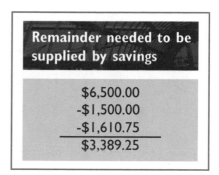

Remainder needed to be supplied by savings

$6,500.00
-$1,500.00
-$1,610.75
———————
$3,389.25

This means that Jackie must have put enough money away in her savings to equal an amount that, with interest, will provide her with $3,389.25 during her retirement years.

What comes next? Yes. Another formula for me and another Quick Chart for you. As you may have guessed, coming up with this figure is just the reverse of the calculation used to figure what Jackie's $250,000.00 was going to be worth to her. In that calculation, we had the principal amount and needed the monthly value. In this case, we have the monthly amount and need to come up with the principal amount.

As has been the case, I have done the math for you. Take a gander at Quick Chart #4 on page 154.

QUICK CHART #4
Sum Required to Provide Savings Income Monthly Payment (for 25 years)

Savings Income	Interest Rate					
	4%	6%	8%	10%	12%	14%
$500.00	$94,726.24	$77,603.43	$64,782.26	$55,023.62	$47,473.28	$41,536.48
$1,000.00	$189,452.48	$155,206.86	$129,564.52	$110,047.23	$94,946.55	$83,072.97
$1,500.00	$284,178.72	$232,810.30	$194,346.78	$165,070.85	$142,419.83	$124,609.45
$2,000.00	$378,904.97	$310,413.73	$259,129.05	$220,094.46	$189,893.10	$166,145.93
$2,500.00	$473,631.21	$388,017.16	$323,911.31	$275,118.08	$237,366.38	$207,682.41
$3,000.00	$568,357.45	$465,620.59	$388,693.57	$330,141.69	$284,839.65	$249,218.90
$3,389.25	$642,054.46	$525,996.06	$439,094.17	$372,950.06	$321,773.86	$281,534.28
$3,500.00	$663,083.69	$543,224.02	$453,475.83	$385,165.31	$332,312.93	$290,755.38
$4,000.00	$757,809.93	$620,827.46	$518,258.09	$440,188.92	$379,786.21	$332,291.86
$5,000.00	$947,226.41	$776,034.32	$647,822.61	$550,236.15	$474,732.76	$415,364.83

The chart shows that $525,996.06 must be accumulated in order to provide Jackie the savings income required ($3,389.25, at 6% interest) per month for the duration of her retirement (25 years).

Are we done? Not quite. Now we know that Jackie needs to have an extra $525,000.00 (roughly) saved before age 65 to realize her retirement goals. How does she do this? What must she put away on a monthly basis in order to have saved the $525,000 by retirement? Another Quick Chart? Nope. Aren't you weary of charts? Didn't we already work with a Quick Chart that enables us to determine the monthly savings amount necessary to achieve a given principal amount after the designated time? I think we did. In fact, I believe it was Quick Chart #2. Review it again on page 149.

Does $525,000.00 appear on the chart as a savings sum on the left of the chart? Yep. Is there a column representing our interest rate of 6%? Yep. Find where the column and the row meet and what do you get? I come up with $522.64. Is that what you got? Good.

So, Jackie needs to put away that amount ($522.64) monthly and invest it at 6% to have the last chunk of retirement money necessary to support her during her golden years. Jackie is on her way.

Now, it is your turn to determine if you will reach your goal.

"Save money and money will save you."
Jamaican saying

Planning to Reach Your Destination

**Exercise 8.1: Choosing Your Financial Professional
(one hour of research, plus visits)**

You will need a financial professional to help you determine how much money you will need at retirement. There is no one-size-fits-all formula. There are too many personal variables involved in determining the amount that will work for you. The following are some factors that have to be taken into account:

○ Current and anticipated lifestyle

○ Children's educational needs

○ Health of the individual(s)

○ Existence or absence of certain large debt at retirement (e.g. mortgage loans)

○ Anticipated dependents at retirement

○ Current and future rates of inflation

Professional Financial Consultants/Planners make their living calculating retirement numbers for people. Your accountant can help you through the math. Same with an Investment Advisor. If you are looking only to ascertain your retirement number, your accountant may be the best source. Beware the counsel of Investment Advisors/Planners/Consultants, who want to sell you products and services that you may not be ready to purchase, in exchange for calculating this number.

Financial professionals fall into three main groups: Accountants (CPA's), Financial Consultants and Investment Advisors. Choosing your financial professionals is as important to your financial wellbeing as your medical professionals are to your physical health. In other words, you should put the same amount of care and effort into selecting your CPA's, FA's and IA's as you do your MD's.

Listed below are some guidelines to consider when establishing (or maintaining) a relationship with financial professionals:

Exercise 8.1 CONTINUED

○ Do they belong to the respective professional trade organization for their expertise?

○ Can they provide references?

○ Are they actually "professional?" Do they handle themselves appropriately when you are in their company?

○ Do they conduct their business with a sense of objectivity and independence or are they just trying to sell you something?

○ Do they take into consideration your personal financial situation, or are they trying to pigeonhole you?

○ Is their fee reasonably matched with your ability to pay?

○ Are they timely in getting information or advice back to you?

○ How is their overall customer service? When you call their office, can you generally speak with them personally?

○ Are they reassuring about your personal financial situation — understanding of the importance of your starting place and direction?

○ Do you match on a personality basis? Do you feel comfortable talking to them about your financial position and goals?

○ Bottom line: DO YOU TRUST THEM? Intuition is a very powerful force. If you do not feel comfortable, get out of the relationship and find someone else to help you.

If you do want to attempt to make the retirement calculations, use one of the many Internet web sites dedicated to this function. The American Association for Retired Persons (www.aarp.org) will provide the information you need.

Planning to Reach Your Destination

Exercise 8.2: Calculating Your Monthly Savings Requirement (45 minutes)

You will need to do the following:

1. Like Jackie, consult a financial professional or make use of a retirement calculator web site to estimate the monthly income you will need to live on when you retire (Retirement Income).

2. Ask your employer to estimate what monies you can reasonably expect to receive from your 401(k) account or other retirement plans (Pension Sum).

3. Consult your Social Security Administration (SSA) benefits statement (or contact the Administration) for the estimate of future monthly income from this source (SSA Income).

4. Use Quick Chart #3 to determine the monthly value you can expect to be provided from your 401(k) during retirement (Pension Income).

5. Subtract your SSA Income and your Pension Income from your Retirement Income:
   [Retirement Income - (SSA Income + Pension Income)]

6. This provides you with your Savings Income amount.

7. Use Quick Chart #4 to find the amount of money you must have saved by retirement (Savings Sum) in order to provide your Savings Income.

8. Use Quick Chart #2 to find the amount of money you will have to invest independently on a monthly basis to augment your SSA benefits and your Pension Income.

9. If the amount of money you need to invest monthly is too large for your current budget to handle, you will have to consider increasing the number of years before your retirement or do more work on optimizing your income and reducing your expenses.

Exercise 8.2 CONTINUED

Now you are finally done — or are you? If you planted an acorn with the hope that it would eventually grow into a strong oak tree, would you plant it and then forget it? Maybe, but wouldn't it have a better chance of survival if you looked after it in its youth by watering it and fertilizing it and generally helping it along its life journey?

Your financial journey deserves no less attention. Lives change in many ways, especially financial situations. You should re-evaluate your financial situation and journey on a periodic basis for two reasons:

○ If there is no significant change in your financial situation, you can derive pleasure in knowing that you are still on track to meet your goals.
○ If a change has occurred and some of your financial assumptions are no longer true, it will be necessary for you to re-evaluate the map of your financial journey. The good news is that you have already done it once — it will be much easier on any subsequent go-around.

I would suggest taking a look every six months or so — unless an obvious change occurs to dictate you doing it sooner.

Note: Some of the more sophisticated retirement calculator web sites will actually perform all the calculations mentioned above. You just need to have your specific data (i.e. SSA contribution, 401(k) lump sum, etc) ready when using the web sites.

Planning to Reach Your Destination

Exercise 8.3: Establish Your Weight Loss Goals (30 minutes)

I'm going to assume that you don't want to spend the rest of your life reaching your weight goal! However, here is where I do want you to plan a realistic time-line for achieving your weight loss.

First I want you to consider carefully: how much weight do you lose per week — NOW, at your present age, not when you were 25! (I can only lose an average of one pound per week, so it will take me a minimum of five months to reach my goal.)

Write your responses to the following in your journal:

○ Expected weight loss per week.

○ Now, in addition, remember that your weight is a symptom. What is your weight a symptom of?

○ How are you going to address this symptom on an ongoing basis?

○ The new diet research recommends that losing 10% of your weight is a realistic percentage and also sufficient to bring you the necessary health benefits. How much is 10% for you?

○ How much time do you need to reach your weight loss goals?

Planning to Reach Your Destination

**Exercise 8.4: Other Benefits of the Weight Loss Program
(20 minutes)**

Besides what it says on the scales, what results do you seek? (For example, going down two sizes, being able to tie your shoe laces, taking strain off your back, knees and feet, more energy.)

It is important to measure reaching your destination not only in terms of an actual weight, but other quantifiable rewards. Make a list, in your journal, of the psychological, emotional, mental and physical rewards you will gain, for example: self-esteem, self-respect, sense of accomplishment, improved health.

Add to this list every time you think of another reward.

Put check marks next to the listed item every time you experience that reward.

Planning to Reach Your Destination

Exercise 8.5: Planning for Moments of Failure (30 minutes)

Let's be honest. We are not machines and we are going to go off track. That is not the important truth. The important truth is having a way to get back on track, seeing as you know in advance, that you are going to wander from the path.

What are the circumstances and triggers that will most likely pull you off course?

Write a list in a column down the left-hand margin of the page. On the right, write down ways you can think of for coping with those triggers and for minimizing their effect. Leave space for later additions. Like this:

Trigger	Coping Mechanisms
Weddings and Parties	Eat beforehand so I'm not hungry
	Eat salads first to take the edge off my hunger
	Strictly no sugar or carbohydrate
Restaurants	Don't think of this as a special occasion and a time to treat myself
	No fried foods
	Decide in advance what I'm going to choose
	No impulse ordering

How are you going to support yourself when you do go off course?

How are you going to get back on course? Write down as many ideas as you can think of and leave space for more.

Planning to Reach Your Destination

Exercise 8.6: Establishing Your Destination (60 minutes)

When it comes to weight loss, your destination isn't a number — it is a sustainable way of life. Write a detailed description of how you want your life to look in terms of your routine and relationship with weight, food, eating patterns and exercise. Include the following:

○ Your personal philosophy of life

○ Atmosphere around food and meal times

○ Cooking and shopping habits

○ Ways of treating and rewarding yourself

○ Quantity and quality of food and beverages consumed

○ Ways of celebrating

○ Ongoing ways of addressing the stresses of life and other triggers that cause weight gain

Action Notes

9
keeping
life in Balance

"There are two things
to aim for in life:
first to get what you want,
and after that to enjoy it.
Only the wisest of mankind
achieve the second."

Logan Pearsall Smith

You can never be too thin or too rich. Right? Wrong!

Our quest is definitely not to become extreme in an opposite direction. Being overweight is dangerous to your health and even life threatening. Likewise, being too thin can be dangerous to health, even life threatening. As a daily matter, being obsessed with weight can and does interfere with the quality of your life. Sometimes you do want to celebrate with a feast or indulge in an ice cream. This is not the same as being addicted to food and eating for the wrong reasons. There can be equally wrong reasons for being thin as for being fat.

Do we even need to go through the dangers and pitfalls of being extreme about gaining money? Probably not. But for the sake of completion, let's remember that an obsession with money can also endanger your health and detract from the quality of life. It can lead to excessive indulgence in stress-related activities such as smoking, caffeine, alcohol, exhaustion and the illnesses associated, like heart disease.

If you are obsessed with gaining money, you are probably so absorbed in work that you do not spend enough time with your family, taking vacations and enjoying leisure activities.

What we want to achieve for ourselves with the **Lose Weight, Gain Money Program**SM is the ability to invest money in ourselves, not the ability to invest ourselves in money!

Remember also, that man does not live by bread alone. You don't only need money to pay your bills — you need money to educate yourself and be the person you want to be. Likewise, we don't eat only for nourishment. We do eat for pleasure — to enjoy the art and taste of good cooking as well as enjoy the social interaction of breaking bread with friends and family.

There will be times when you need to spend a chunk of money or take out a loan. There are different phases in our lives and some are more expensive than others. For example, if you are in your forties, you are in one of the most expensive phases of your life: saving for your children's college education, saving for retirement and meeting all the expenses of bringing up, sheltering and feeding a family.

Keeping Life in Balance

As you work through the program, hold the intention of establishing balance in your life.

What Is Balance?

Recently I listened to a client telling me how she was going to work even harder for the next three years so that she could pay off her debt — and then relax. This client already has heart problems and seems to me to be continually exhausted. I shuddered at the thought of her working even harder and literally feared for her life. I didn't want to scare her, but she had just scared me.

"What if there isn't anyone there in three years time who can relax?" I asked.

"What are you saying?" she asked.

"That you're already on the edge and you need to reconsider. I want you to go and think about how life would look if you allowed yourself five years to pay off the debt. Perhaps you could start to relax now and pay off your debt. That would be more balanced."

Two weeks later this client reported to me that she had reflected on her situation and had realized that she should give herself more time to pay off the debt. She had also decided to take another course (load software) that would train her in more effective handling of the financial side of her business.

In our society, we have curious programs for keeping our lives in balance. We work hard. Then we play hard. We see-saw from one extreme to another. That is not true balance. Balance is when the see-saw stays level because equal weight is placed at each end. That will cause stasis, which will bore us and cause us to jump off — really unbalancing the equation. We are better off thinking about how to keep the see-saw gently moving through a comfortable range of the arc, ensuring that each side gets its fair share of weight.

For example, if you work hard during the week, take the whole weekend off. Once every three months take a long weekend and go away with the spouse and children, or just rest!

Establishing Balance in Your Life

**Exercise 9.1: What a Balanced Lifestyle Means for You.
(30 minutes)**

Take time to reflect on what a balanced lifestyle means for you personally.

Make notes in your journal.

Assess how you live your life and how to create balance. See how you can modify your lifestyle to maintain balance on an ongoing basis. (Daily reflection for one week.)

Here are some questions to assist you:

○ How much time do you spend at work?

○ How much time do you spend with your family?

○ How much time do you spend with your friends?

○ How much time do you spend following your interests/hobby?

○ How much time do you spend exercising?

○ How much time do you spend maintaining your home and yard?

○ How much time do you spend learning?

○ How much time do you spend resting?

○ How much time do you spend processing your emotions?

○ How much time do you spend in reflection/following your spiritual practice?

○ Are you getting enough sleep?

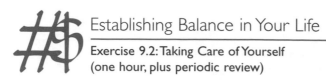

Establishing Balance in Your Life

Exercise 9.2: Taking Care of Yourself
(one hour, plus periodic review)

You have seven major chakras and each one needs attention on an ongoing basis. Here is a review:

Layers of Your Self		
Chakra	**Area**	**Kind of Attention**
Root	Physical	Diet and Exercise
Sacral	Emotions	Family, Friends, Emotional Processing
Solar Plexus	Will, Money	Work
Heart	Love	Family, Friends, Volunteer Work
Throat	Self-Expression	Art, Music, Writing, Singing, Courses
Third Eye	Intuition	Meditation, Meditative Movement, Listening to Music, Unstructured Time
Crown	Intellect & Spirit	Courses, Training, Spiritual Practice

Think about each chakra in turn, and note in your journal:

○ How do you pay attention to each aspect of yourself?

○ What would you like to add?

The Science of Contentment

As you wrestle with the difficulties of creating balance in your life, you will no doubt find yourself confronted by all the choices — another symptom of our excessive culture.

Incarnating in the U.S.A. (or another wealthy westernized culture) automatically brings with it the need to resolve your spiritual issues around wealth and abundance, because this is the wealthiest and most abundant country in the world.

To establish your priorities, remember who you are: **you as an individual.** What is really important to you? What do you want your life to be about? When you are on your deathbed, what do you want to look back and see? How do you want your family and friends to remember you?

Once you have established your priorities in life, you have a way of measuring your choices: Do they serve your priorities or do they hinder your priorities?

Each of us must decide for ourselves. Do not judge yourself harshly if all you want is a two-room cabin in the woods. Nor do you need to judge yourself if what you want is three homes, eight cars, three race horses and a yacht. But do ascertain what is enough for you — and be sure to load the software and enter the data that will yield this result.

 ## Establishing Balance in Your Life

Exercise 9.3: List Your Priorities (one hour)

What is important to you?

Write a list of your priorities in your journal and leave space for future additions. Refer to this list whenever you are confused, needing to make a decision or feeling off-track.

* * *

Our greatest hope is that every reader of this book will be free of ever having to worry again about weight or money.

We began this book by looking at seven behavioral similarities between weight gain and money loss that can lure us into a downward spiral of self - destruction. We ascertained that weight gain and money loss were both the results of our lifestyles and that if we wanted to change either one or both, we needed to make systematic, supported changes in our lifestyles.

You have been doing the program for twelve weeks now and should have all your initial building blocks in place. Is that it? Definitely not!

○ Review the contents of your journal — which has become a precious document

○ Go back to the beginning of the book and begin the cycle again

That is how you will reverse the downward spiral of weight gain and money loss. Continue following the **Lose Weight, Gain Money**℠ program, constantly refining the process, and integrating the knowledge into your daily life.

Action Notes

Appendix A: Additional Quick Charts

The following Quick Charts, as well as those in the text, are designed to guide your general thinking about finances. We highly recommend that you consult your financial professional to get accurate information about your specific financial situation. The spirit of this program has been to encourage you to take responsibility for your personal well-being and put together a team of professionals to assist and support you in the necessary areas of expertise.

Additional Quick Charts, as well as interactive calculators are available at our web site www.loseweightgainmoney.com. You can perform even more detailed calculations using the financial calculators on the AARP website www.aarp.org.

Use these Quick Charts in the same manner as those in the body of the book. If you find the numbers for which you need an answer are not in the left-hand column, you can use simple addition on the amounts that are there to come up with your numbers.

For example, in Quick Chart #2 (15 years), if you find that your Savings Sum number is $1,500,000.00 (which isn't on the chart) you can simply take the value for $1,000,000.00 ($3,438.57, at 6%) and add it to the value for $500,000.00 at the same interest rate (here $1,719.28) for a total of $5,157.85.

In a similar fashion, if your Desired Return is halfway between two numbers on the chart, simply add the chart value for the two numbers on the chart, then divide by 2.

Your Desired Return: $75,000.00 (15 years at 6%)

Chart entry for $100,000.00:	$343.86
Chart entry for $50,000.00:	+ $171.93
Sum	$515.79
Divided by 2	$257.90 (rounded)

QUICK CHART #2
Monthly Investment Needed To Return A Savings Sum In 15 Years At A Given Investment Rate

Savings Sum	Interest Rate					
	4%	6%	8%	10%	12%	14%
$50,000.00	$203.18	$171.93	$144.49	$120.64	$100.08	$82.54
$100,000.00	$406.35	$343.86	$288.99	$241.27	$200.17	$165.07
$150,000.00	$609.53	$515.79	$433.48	$361.91	$300.25	$247.61
$200,000.00	$812.71	$687.71	$577.97	$482.54	$400.34	$330.15
$250,000.00	$1,015.89	$859.64	$722.46	$603.18	$500.42	$412.69
$300,000.00	$1,219.06	$1,031.57	$866.96	$723.82	$600.50	$495.22
$350,000.00	$1,422.24	$1,203.50	$1,011.45	$844.45	$700.59	$577.76
$400,000.00	$1,625.42	$1,375.43	$1,155.94	$965.09	$800.67	$660.30
$500,000.00	$2,031.77	$1,719.28	$1,444.93	$1,206.36	$1,000.84	$825.37
$750,000.00	$3,047.66	$2,578.93	$2,167.39	$1,809.54	$1,501.26	$1,238.06
$1,000,000.00	$4,063.55	$3,438.57	$2,889.85	$2,412.72	$2,001.68	$1,650.75
$1,250,000.00	$5,079.43	$4,298.21	$3,612.32	$3,015.90	$2,502.10	$2,063.43

QUICK CHART #2
Monthly Investment Needed To Return A Savings Sum In 20 Years At A Given Investment Rate

Savings Sum	Interest Rate					
	4%	6%	8%	10%	12%	14%
$50,000.00	$136.32	$108.22	$84.89	$65.84	$50.54	$38.43
$100,000.00	$204.49	$162.32	$127.33	$98.77	$75.81	$57.64
$150,000.00	$272.65	$216.43	$169.77	$131.69	$101.09	$76.85
$200,000.00	$408.97	$324.65	$254.66	$197.53	$151.63	$115.28
$250,000.00	$545.29	$432.86	$339.55	$263.38	$202.17	$153.71
$300,000.00	$681.62	$541.08	$424.43	$329.22	$252.72	$192.14
$350,000.00	$817.94	$649.29	$509.32	$395.06	$303.26	$230.56
$400,000.00	$1,090.59	$865.72	$679.09	$526.75	$404.34	$307.42
$500,000.00	$1,363.23	$1,082.16	$848.87	$658.44	$505.43	$384.27
$750,000.00	$2,044.85	$1,623.23	$1,273.30	$987.66	$758.15	$576.41
$1,000,000.00	$2,726.47	$2,164.31	$1,697.73	$1,316.88	$1,010.86	$768.54
$1,250,000.00	$3,408.09	$2,705.39	$2,122.17	$1,646.10	$1,263.58	$960.68

QUICK CHART #3
Monthly Return Of Lump Sum Over 15 Years At Selected Interest Rate

Lump Sum	Interest Rate					
	4%	6%	8%	10%	12%	14%
$100,000.00	$739.69	$843.86	$955.65	$1,074.61	$1,200.17	$1,331.74
$150,000.00	$1,109.53	$1,265.79	$1,433.48	$1,611.91	$1,800.25	$1,997.61
$200,000.00	$1,479.38	$1,687.71	$1,911.30	$2,149.21	$2,400.34	$2,663.48
$250,000.00	$1,849.22	$2,109.64	$2,389.13	$2,686.51	$3,000.42	$3,329.35
$300,000.00	$2,219.06	$2,531.57	$2,866.96	$3,223.82	$3,600.50	$3,995.22
$350,000.00	$2,588.91	$2,953.50	$3,344.78	$3,761.12	$4,200.59	$4,661.09
$400,000.00	$2,958.75	$3,375.43	$3,822.61	$4,298.42	$4,800.67	$5,326.97
$450,000.00	$3,328.60	$3,797.36	$4,300.43	$4,835.72	$5,400.76	$5,992.84
$500,000.00	$3,698.44	$4,219.28	$4,778.26	$5,373.03	$6,000.84	$6,658.71
$1,000,000.00	$7,396.88	$8,438.57	$9,556.52	$10,746.05	$12,001.68	$13,317.41

QUICK CHART #3
Monthly Return Of Lump Sum Over 20 Years At Selected Interest Rate

Lump Sum	Interest Rate					
	4%	6%	8%	10%	12%	14%
$100,000.00	$605.98	$716.43	$836.44	$965.02	$1,101.09	$1,243.52
$150,000.00	$908.97	$1,074.65	$1,254.66	$1,447.53	$1,651.63	$1,865.28
$200,000.00	$1,211.96	$1,432.86	$1,672.88	$1,930.04	$2,202.17	$2,487.04
$250,000.00	$1,514.95	$1,791.08	$2,091.10	$2,412.55	$2,752.72	$3,108.80
$300,000.00	$1,817.94	$2,149.29	$2,509.32	$2,895.06	$3,303.26	$3,730.56
$350,000.00	$2,120.93	$2,507.51	$2,927.54	$3,377.58	$3,853.80	$4,352.32
$400,000.00	$2,423.92	$2,865.72	$3,345.76	$3,860.09	$4,404.34	$4,974.08
$450,000.00	$2,726.91	$3,223.94	$3,763.98	$4,342.60	$4,954.89	$5,595.84
$500,000.00	$3,029.90	$3,582.16	$4,182.20	$4,825.11	$5,505.43	$6,217.60
$1,000,000.00	$6,059.80	$7,164.31	$8,364.40	$9,650.22	$11,010.86	$12,435.21

Appendix B: Resource List

The Lose Weight, Gain Money℠ Program
www.loseweightgainmoney.com

References (Alphabetized by Author)

DIET

The South Beach Diet: The Delicious, Doctor-Designed, Foolproof Plan for Fast and Healthy Weight Loss
Arthur Agatston • Rodale Press • 2003

Dr. Atkins' New Diet Revolution
Robert C. Atkins • Avon • 2001

Eat Right for Your Type
Peter J. D'Adamo • Putnam Pub Group • 1996

The Ultimate Weight Solution: The 7 Keys to Weight Loss Freedom
Phil MacGraw • Free Press • 2003

The 5 Day Miracle Diet:
Adele Puhn, M.S., C.N.S. • Ballantine Books • 1996

The Midlife Miracle Diet: Tame Your Insulin Resistance
Adele Puhn, M.S., C.N.S. • Viking • 2003

HOW TO CHANGE

Love Is In the Earth: A Kaleidoscope of Crystals
Melody • Earth-Love Publishing House • 1995

Go Up and Seek God
Vianna Stibal • Rolling Thunder • 1998

Go Up and Work With God
Vianna Stibal • Rolling Thunder • 2000

Homeopathy A-Z
Dana Ullman • Hay House • 2002

The Complete Book of Essential Oils & Aromatherapy
Valerie Ann Worwood • New World Library • 1991

MONEY/INVESTING

Your Money or Your Life: Transforming Your Relationship with Money and Achieving Financial Independence
Joe Dominquez; Vicki Robin • Penguin USA • 1999

9 Steps to Financial Freedom
Suze Orman • Three Rivers Press • 2000

Wealth Happens One Day At a Time: 365 Days to a Brighter Financial Future
Brooke M. Stephens • HarperBusiness • 2000

The Soul of Money: Transforming Your Relationship with Money and Life
Lynne Twist; Teresa Barker • W. W. Norton & Company • 2003

Making the Most of your Money
Jane Bryant Quinn • Simon & Schuster • 1977

HOW TO CHANGE

The Use of the Self
F.M. Alexander • Orion • 2002

The Act of Living
Walter Carrington • Mornun Time Press • 1999

The Complete Illustrated Guide to the Alexander Technique: A Practical Program for Health, Poise and Fitness
Glynn MacDonald • Elements Books Limited • 1998

Web Sites

DIET (Alphabetized by Name)

3 Fat Chicks www.3fatchicks.com

Dieter's Club www.dietersclub.com

Macrobiotics www.kushiinstitute.org
www.macroamerica.com
www.macrobioticmeals.com

My Diet Buddy www.mydietbuddy.com

Ornish, Dean www.webmd.com
www.pmri.org
www.lifestyleadvantage.org

Overeaters Anonymous www.oa.org

Puhn, Adele www.adelepuhn.com

Weight Watchers www.weightwatchers.com

MONEY/INVESTING (Alphabetized by Name)

AARP www.aarp.org • Phone (800) 424-3410

AAII www.aaii.com • Phone (800) 428-2244
 (American Association of Individual Investors)

Banksite www.banksite.com

Debtors Anonymous www.debtorsanonymous.org

Debt Support Group www.ivillage.com/money/life_stage/deepdebt

Motley Fool www.fool.com

Social Security Administration www.ssa.gov • Phone (800) 772-1213

HOW TO CHANGE (Alphabetized by Subject)

Acupuncture
American Academy of Medical Acupuncture www.medicalacupunture.org
 Phone (323) 937-5514

Alexander Technique
American Society for Teachers of the Alexander Technique
 www.alexandertech.org • Phone (800) 473-0620, (413) 584-2359

Aromatherapy
Aromatherapy: Kamala Perfumes www.kamala.com • Phone(847) 424-1963

The National Association for Holistic Aromatherapy www.naha.org
 Phone (888) ASK-NAHA, (206) 547-2164

Astrology
Association for Astrological Networking www.afan.org
 Phone (212) 726-1407, (800) 578-AFAN

The American Federation of Astrologers www.astrologers.com
 Phone (480) 838-1751, (888) 301-7630

Body-Mind Centering
The School for Body-Mind Centering www.bodymindcentering.com
 Phone (413) 256-8615

Chiropractic

The Council on Chiropractic Education (CCE) www.CCE-USA.org
Phone(480) 443-8877

International Chiropractors Association www.chiropractic.org
Phone (800) 423-4690, (703)528-5000

Coaching

Brian Tracy International www.briantracy.com • Phone (858) 481-2977

International Coach Federation www.coachfederation.org
Phone (888) 423-3131or (202) 712-9039

Color Therapy

Color Therapy Center www.colortherapycenter.com Phone (813) 323-4944

Colour Energy for Body and Soul www.colourenergy.com
Phone (604) 687-3757, (800) 225-1226

Craniosacral Therapy

The Craniosacral Therapy Association of North America
www.craniosacraltherapy.org

Crystals

The Association of Melody Crystal Healing Instructors (TAOMCHI)
www.taomchi.com

Dance

International Somatic Movement Education & Therapy Association
www.ismeta.org • Phone (212) 229-7666

American Dance Therapy Association www.adta.org • Phone(410) 997-4040

DNA Reprogramming

Vianna Stibal, Vianna's Natures Path www.thetahealing.com
Phone (208) 524-0808

Exercise

American College of Sports Medicine www.acsm.org

American Council on Exercise www.acefitness.org

Feldenkrais

Feldenkrais Guild of North America www.feldenkrais.com
Phone (800) 775-2118, (503) 221-6612

Feng Shui

American Feng Shui Institute www.amfengshui.com • Phone (626) 571-2757

International Feng Shui Guild www.fengshuiguild.com • Phone (954) 345-3838

Flower Essences

International Association of Flower Essence Producers
  www.floweressenceproducers.org • Phone (907) 235-2188

Perelandra www.perelandra-ltd.com • Phone (800) 960-8806, (540) 937-2153

Healing

FourWinds Academy for the Healing Arts and Sciences
  www.4windsacademy.org

Barbara Brennan School of Healing www.barbarabrennan.com
  Phone (800) 924-2564, (561) 620-8767

Rosalyn Bruyere www.rosalynbruyere.org • Phone (626) 306-2170

Caroline Myss Education Institute www.myss.com • Phone (847) 266-8630

Healing Touch International www.htifoundation.org • Phone (281) 856-8340

Herbalism

A Journal for the Clinical Practitioner www.medherb.com

Homeopathy

North American Society of Homeopaths www.homeopathy.org
  Phone (206) 720-7000

National Center for Homeopathy www.homeopathic.org
  Phone (877) 624-0613

Karate

United States Karate Alliance www.uska.net • Phone (505) 872-1091

USA National Karate-do Federation www.usankf.org • Phone (206) 440-8386

Massage Therapy

Commission on Massage Therapy Accreditation www.comta.org
  Phone (847) 869-5039

Naturopathic Medicine

Naturopathic Medicine Network www.pandamedicine.com

Past-Life Regression

Brian Weiss, M.D., The Weiss Institute www.brianweiss.com
  Phone (305) 598-8151

Pilates www.pilatesmethodalliance.org

Reflexology

Reflexology Association of America www.reflexology-usa.org

Reflexology Institute www.reflexologyinstitute.com
  Phone (800) 533-1837, (303) 237-1530

Reiki

The International Center for Reiki Training www.reiki.org
   Phone (800) 332-8112, (248) 948-8112

International Association of Reiki Professionals www.iarp.org
   Phone (603) 881-8838

Reiki Council www.reikicouncil.com • Phone (630) 926-5891

Rolfing

The Rolfing Institute of Structural Integration www.rolf.org
   Phone (800) 530-8875, (303) 449-5903

Taekwondo

United States Taekwondo Won www.ustw.org • Phone (513) 791-8888

Tai Chi

Tai Chi Magazine www.tai-chi.com
   Phone (800) 888-9119, (323) 665-7773

Trager Approach

The Trager Approach www.trager.com • Phone (216) 896-9383

Yoga

Anusara Yoga www.anusarayoga.com
   Phone (888) 398-9642, (281)367-9763

Yoga International www.yimag.org

Yoga Journal www.yogajournal.com

Action Notes

Action Notes

Want a new perspective on your life? Vivien shares her healing journey, beginning in Apartheid-stricken South Africa and ending in the United States, with her vision of FourWinds Academy, a college for training professional healers. *Everyday Magic* is an easy way to find out about nutrition, crystals, spirit guides, past-lives, the Alexander Technique and many other healing modalities and is guaranteed to inspire you on your own path to health, abundance and love. See our website for more information www.everydaymagic.us.

A practical manual on how to build a private practice and client-based small business. The author, Vivien Schapera, has been in private practice for 20 years and shares the steps she took to establish her practice first in South Africa, and then in the U.S. This handbook identifies the additional skills required, beyond professional expertise, to be successfully self-employed, explains the word-of-mouth process and how to stimulate and support this most important key to attracting clients. Each chapter ends with an easy to-do list guaranteed to empower the reader.

Pausing, noticing, directing and allowing are the core mental attentions for daily practice between Alexander Technique lessons. *Guided Lessons* is a big volume, spiral bound at the top, so that pages can be flipped for easy study. Each page is a simple, well-constructed set of directions for performing daily activities with more ease. Photographs and drawings bring the lessons into sharp focus.